Lazarus

A Contemporary Reading of John 11:1-46

Zacchaeus Studies: New Testament

General Editor: Mary Ann Getty

Lazarus

A Contemporary Reading of John 11:1-46

by

Brendan Byrne, S.J.

A Michael Glazier Book
THE LITURGICAL PRESS
Collegeville, Minnesota

In memory of

John J. Scullion, S.J.

who entered the fullness
of eternal life.

November 24, 1990

Typography by Brenda Belizzone and Mary Brown.

1	2	3	4	5	6	7	8	9

Library of Congress Cataloging-in-Publication Data

Byrne, Brendan, S.J.
    Lazarus : a contemporary reading of John 11:1-46 / by Brendan
Byrne.
        p.   cm. — (Zacchaeus studies. New Testament)
    "A Michael Glazier book."
    Includes bibliographical references.
    ISBN 0-8146-5657-9
    1. Bible. N.T. John XI, 1-46—Criticism, interpretation, etc.
  2. Raising of Lazarus (Miracle) 3. Lazarus, of Bethany, Saint.
  I. Title. II. Series.
  BS2615.2.B97 1990
  226.7'06—dc20   90-44274
                                                      CIP

Contents

Editor's Note

Zacchaeus Studies provide concise, readable and relatively inexpensive scholarly studies on particular aspects of scripture and theology. The New Testament section of the series presents studies dealing with focal or debated questions; and the volumes focus on specific texts or particular themes of current interest in biblical interpretation. Specialists have their professional journals and other forums where they discuss matters of mutual concern, exchange ideas and further contemporary trends of research; and some of their work on contemporary biblical research is now made accessible for students and others in *Zacchaeus Studies*.

The authors in this series share their own scholarship in non-technical language, in the areas of their expertise and interest. These writers stand with the best in current biblical scholarship in the English-speaking world. Since most of them are teachers, they are accustomed to presenting difficult material in comprehensible form without compromising a high level of critical judgment and analysis.

The works of this series are ecumenical in content and purpose and cross credal boundaries. They are designed to augment formal and informal biblical study and discussion. Hopefully they will also serve as texts to enhance and supplement seminary, university and college classes. The series will also aid Bible study groups, adult education and parish religious education classes to develop intelligent, versatile and challenging programs for those they serve.

Mary Ann Getty
New Testament Editor

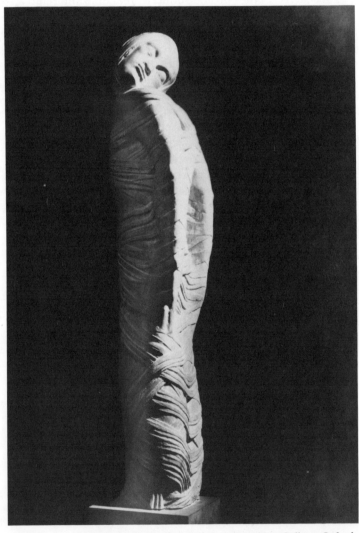

Lazarus by Sir Jacob Epstein, courtesy New College, Oxford.

Introduction

The large antechapel of New College, Oxford, is bare save for a most striking sculpture that immediately captures and then holds the visitor's eye. It is a sculpture of Lazarus. The figure stands upright, but is still so tightly bound all over with the winding-cloths of death as to present a study of total helplessness and passivity. Only the head is beginning to move, tilted slightly backwards and across the shoulder, responding, it would seem, to some call that is coming from behind. Behind stretches the main body of the chapel—the long row of choir stalls and finally the altar and great lectern from where the gospel is proclaimed. As one enters the ancient chapel, nothing could more powerfully symbolize the truth that what one approaches this church to hear is the word of Christ, always summoning from death to life. Despite its name, New College is actually very old; the sculpture, by comparison, quite recent. The combination perfectly asserts that the gospel heard in this ancient place is still a life-giving word for today.

Epstein's "Lazarus" in its New College setting serves as a reminder of the power the story of the raising of Lazarus in John 11 has exercised in Christian faith and imagination down the centuries. Lazarus has been depicted in art, in drama and poetry. Even those sceptical that any historical reality underlies the story find that it exercises a powerful imaginative appeal. It taps into the most pervasive and ancient fear of all—the fear of death, of extinction.[1] Lazarus remains a symbol of defiance, of acceptance of death and yet its overthrow. The story touches the central focus of all religions and much modern philosophic enquiry: how to bear the end of life, how to live with the prospect of dying.[2]

Granted this universal appeal of the Lazarus motif, the central focus of this present study lies upon the story in its original setting in the Gospel of John. My aim is to render accessible the fruits of modern scholarship upon a biblical text of central and lasting interest. The interpretative method lying behind the study is basically that of historical and literary criticism. I am aware that the Lazarus story lends itself to a variety of interpretative method and that methods other than the historical critical have been fruitfully employed.[3] But experience of teaching and discussing the Gospel of John with a considerable variety of people has convinced me that a study of John 11:1-46 in its original setting, particularly a study which attends seriously to the literary structure of the final text, provides a rich basis for contemporary meaning. The concerns which exercised the Johannine community, in particular those which seem to underlie the composition of John 11, are basically the same as those which exercise believers today. How death can be reconciled with faith in a loving and life-giving God, how grief and anger at death can be incorporated into a living faith: these are the perennial questions which the span of centuries does not alter. In particular, it seems to me, the whole presentation of the Lazarus story in John 11 has much to say to the contemporary concern for a biblically based pastoral ministry to the grieving and the dying. This concern will be uppermost as we seek to read John 11 in a way that is both contemporary and faithful in historical critical terms.

Since, as I shall argue, John 11:1-46 is really a microcosm of the entire Gospel of John, it is important from the outset to set it within the framework of the wider gospel. Accordingly, this study begins with a brief account of the community that gave rise to the gospel, the main lines of its view of the Christian faith, and the literary features and techniques characteristic of this gospel. I also attempt at this point to situate the Lazarus episode within the broader "geography" of the entire document. A second chapter takes up the passage in question, John 11:1-46 and enquires into general questions appropriately considered before detailed study of the text: the overall structure of the narrative, the literary form in which it is cast. This preliminary study completed, the way is clear for detailed, section by section study of the text in chap. 3. Following the detailed investigation it is possible to enquire into the origins behind the tradition found in John 11:1-46 and come to some conclusion about the historical status of the miracle story; this is done in chap. 4. Finally, the Conclusion attempts to draw the study together, with particular regard to contemporary meaning.

1

The Raising of Lazarus within
the Wider Pattern of the Gospel

The Fourth Gospel emerged in the final decades of the 1st century, C.E., as the product of a community with a very distinctive experience of the Christian faith. The Gospel itself attributes the origin of its witness and indeed its authorship to a figure whom it names in the final chapters as "the disciple whom Jesus loved." A tradition, going back to the late 2nd century, identifies this "Beloved Disciple" as John, the son of Zebedee, a leading disciple of Jesus. Hence we have the "Gospel according to St. John." Few scholars hold this identification today. Most agree, however, that underlying the somewhat idealized and symbolic figure appearing as the "Beloved Disciple" in the final chapters stands a real historical person, who was probably the founder and head of the Johannine "school" in the period of its consolidation.

It is to this figure, who may have been an eye-witness follower of Jesus, though not one of the Twelve, that Johannine Christianity as reflected in the Gospel and the three Letters (1-3 John) owes its peculiar stamp. The entire Gospel rests upon his sure witness. It even claims that "it is this disciple who has written these things" (21:24). While hardly true in literal terms, the claim shows that it is essentially his experience of Jesus that the community treasured and sought to fix in written form by means of the Gospel.[1]

The Fourth Gospel is, then, essentially the record of a privileged experience of Jesus. Through the witness of the "Beloved Disciple" the Johannine community felt they had an access to the life-giving impact of Jesus in no way inferior to that of the original disciples and eyewitnesses. The essential aim of the Gospel is to preserve this witness for themselves and to offer it to others. We can hear the voice of the community making this offer if we turn to the opening verses of the First Letter of John (1:1-4):

> That which was from the beginning,
> which we have heard,
> which we have seen with our eyes,
> which we have looked upon and
> touched with our hands,
> concerning the word of life -
> the life was made manifest,
> and we saw it, and testify to it,
> and proclaim to you the eternal life
> which was with the Father
> and was made manifest to us -
> that which we have seen and heard
> we proclaim also to you,
> so that you may have fellowship with us;
> and our fellowship is with the Father
> and with his Son Jesus Christ.
> And we are writing this that our joy may be complete.

Earlier, in the Prologue to the Gospel, the evangelist had written, speaking in the name of the community (1:12-14):

> But to all who received him,
> who believed in his name,
> he gave power to become children of God;
> who were born, not of blood,
> nor of the will of the flesh,
> nor of the will of man,
> but of God.
> And the Word became flesh
> and dwelt among us,
> and we have seen his glory,
> glory as of the only-begotten of the Father,
> full of grace and truth.

And concluding the first edition of the Gospel the evangelist wrote (20:30-31):

> Now Jesus did many other signs in the presence
> of the disciples, which are not written in this book;
> but these are written that you may believe
> that Jesus is the Christ, the Son of God, and
> that believing you may have life in his name.

What we have here is something akin to what one finds in the weekend supplements to our daily newspapers. All kinds of groups and communities advertise an experience they wish to share with a wider public: Yoga, or transcendental meditation, Tai Chi, re-birthing or the like. Almost invariably the notice will be accompanied by a statement promising that taking this course, attending this weekend, undergoing this experience, will lead to enhancement of life, indeed to something which in Johannine terms might be described as being "reborn." Each is saying, "We have had this life-giving experience. It has changed our life. It can transform yours. We are offering it to you."

If this is a correct analogy to what the Johannine community was trying to do, then it should be clear that in historical terms the Gospel is operating at two levels. In one sense it is telling the story of Jesus, presenting the Christian experience in terms of his life. It is transporting us back to his times, to the villages and lake-shore of Galilee, to the city and temple of Jerusalem. But in so doing it is not seeking to provide an accurate historical account of Jesus in his time. Rather, the aim is to involve us in the drama of becoming a disciple of Jesus here and now. The Gospel exists to mediate to subsequent generations an experience of Jesus which it firmly believes to be just as valid and life-giving as that of the original disciples.

This is the whole point of the scene with Thomas which forms the culmination of the first edition of the Gospel (20:24-29). "Have you believed because you have seen me?" says Jesus. "Blessed are those who have not seen and yet become believers" (v. 29). Subsequent believers are not in an inferior position. On the contrary, they hear the Lord's special "blessing" upon them. Though they do not literally see and hear and touch like Thomas, through receiving the Gospel in faith they can have an encounter with Jesus in every way as real and life-giving.

So, while telling a story which seems to be "back there," the evangelist is really concerned with what is being offered to his own and subsequent generations. Each reader is invited to take up her or his role in the drama of Jesus: to identify with the attendants at the wedding at Cana, to be the woman at the well of Samaria, to be the blind man enlightened by Jesus, to be Lazarus called forth to life. The saving encounters with Jesus enjoyed by his original disciples are to be had in just as authentic and powerful a way within the life of the Johannine community.

For whom was the Fourth Gospel written? Here again we probably have to reckon with a dual audience. The Gospel contains features suggesting that it was composed to hold out the promise of enhanced life to people who have not yet come to faith in Jesus (cf. esp. 20:30-31). On the other hand, there is much in it to suggest that it is directed also towards strengthening and radicalizing the faith of those who have been believers for some time. These believers find themselves confronted with fresh temptation and challenge as they face the final break with Judaism. They must also come to terms with the continuing "absence" of Jesus and the fact that the ordinary patterns of human life and death continue despite the "eternal life" which they claim to possess as his gift. The Gospel, and particularly the Lazarus sequence, as we shall see, is very much designed to summon up the deeper faith that new situations demand.

What, then, are the principal means, literary and theological, which the Fourth Gospel employs to nourish this deeper faith? For the remainder of this opening chapter I should like to dwell upon these features—in particular upon the Johannine idea of miracle as "sign," the concept of "eternal life," and the more specifically literary techniques of irony, misunderstanding and the interplay between discourse and symbol.

The "Signs" of Jesus in the Fourth Gospel

A particularly distinctive technique of the Fourth Gospel is the presentation of Jesus' miracles in terms of "signs." All four Gospels link the performance of "mighty works" with the ministry of Jesus: the expulsion of demons (exorcisms), healing of the sick, actions that defy the ordinary course of nature such as walking on water or multiplying bread. Already in the synoptic Gospels we find it to be the case that the emphasis is not so much upon the miraculous deed as upon the faith required to appropriate it properly. There is also stress upon what the mighty deed implies with respect to the role and mission of Jesus, specifically in regard to the advent of the Kingdom or Rule of God (Matt 11:4-5; Luke 7:22; Matt 12:28; Luke 11:20).

The Fourth Gospel, it seems, had access to a collection of traditions about Jesus' miracle-working which it shares with the synoptic tradition. Many scholars hold that the account of Jesus' public life found in John 1-12 is largely dependent upon a "Signs-Source," which possibly existed in written form.[2] At an early stage of the tradition "sign" referred especially to a "messianic" work. The chief purpose of the source would have been to demonstrate that Jesus was the Messiah of Jewish expectation.[3] In chap. 7 of John's Gospel we pick up echoes of debates concerning Jesus' messiahship in which his "signs" stand at the forefront: "Yet many of the people believed in him; they said, 'When the Christ appears, will he do more signs than this man has done?'" (v. 31).

In its final form, however, the Fourth Gospel takes us on a more developed exploration of Jesus' miracle-working activity in terms of "sign." Six "works" clearly seem to qualify as signs:

> the changing of water into wine at Cana (2:1-11),
> the healing of the royal official's son (4:46-54),
> the healing of the paralytic at the pool (5:1-9a),
> the feeding of the five thousand (6:1-15),
> the enlightening of the man born blind (9:1-7).
> the raising of Lazarus (11:1-46)

In this list the raising of Lazarus comes as the sixth and culminating sign.[4]

All six signs constitute preliminary revelations of Jesus' glory, leading up to the culminating "moment" of revelation that takes place on the cross. Despite considerable variety in structure and detail, a certain pattern emerges. Each seems to presuppose a twofold level of faith or, more precisely, a progress or "journey" from one level of faith, considered inadequate, to full, radical faith in the Johannine sense. Three "moments" may be discerned in the unfolding of the sign: 1. All begins with the disclosure of the presence of a normal *human need* in some form: the failure of wine at a wedding (chap. 2), the critical illness of a child (end of chap. 4), an almost lifelong paralysis (chap. 5), insufficient food for a great crowd in a remote place (chap. 6), being blind from birth (chap. 9), grave illness ensuing in actual death (chap. 11).

2. The need comes to Jesus' attention and eventually he *remedies it miraculously.* It is characteristic of immature faith that it rests simply at this level of the miraculous and draws from it wrong or inadequate conclusions about Jesus. This is particularly brought out in the sequence in chap. 6, where the crowd, after they have been miraculously fed, see in Jesus "the prophet who is coming into the world" (v. 14). They want to make Jesus their king (v. 15). Their interest in him is basically in one who can constantly and miraculously respond to their everyday needs (v. 34: "Lord, give us this bread always;" cf. v. 26). This "needs-based" faith is prompted by the miracle (cf. Jesus' preliminary taunt to the royal official: "Unless you see signs and wonders you will not believe" [4:48]). True radical faith (the kind the royal official eventually displays [4:50]) precedes the miracle and goes beyond it to penetrate and disclose its full meaning.

3. Thus the third stage of the "sign" is always the *revelation of a new dimension of the divine presence in Jesus.* Jesus is not simply the miraculous provider of bread: he *is* "the Bread of Life" (6:35, 48, 51). He is not merely the restorer of sight (chap. 9); he is the "Light of the world" (1:4; 8:12; 9:4; 12:46). He is not simply the converter of water into wine at a wedding (chap. 2); in his presence there overflows the wine celebrating the eschatological wedding of God and his people. He does not simply overcome physical paralysis (chap. 5); as one who is ever at work, as his Creator Father is "at work," he overcomes the paralysis for which the Jewish Law, symbolized by the five porticos near the Pool, is no match. The bringing back

of Lazarus to this physical, still mortal life (chap. 11) is only a sign of the deeper reality where Jesus is for all believers "the resurrection and the life" (11:25).

In short, then, in the Johannine idea of "sign" the actual miracle is only a means to disclose a deeper reality. Inadequate faith stops at the miracle, because it is content simply with the prospect of remedying ordinary human needs. Adequate or perfect faith goes beyond the miraculous to penetrate the deeper meaning: the presence of God's life-giving revelation in Jesus.

We can perhaps depict the process in the following way:

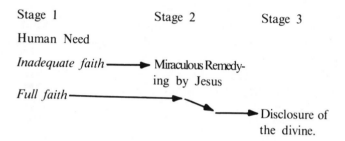

Stage 1   Stage 2   Stage 3

Human Need

Inadequate faith ——→ Miraculous Remedy-
                       ing by Jesus

Full faith ——————→
                          ↘ ——————→ Disclosure of
                                    the divine.

The "signs," then, in the Fourth Gospel stand totally at the service of faith. To some extent they initiate faith - as in the case of the disciples at after the first Cana miracle (2:11; cf. 20:30-31). But the evangelist frequently notes the inadequacy of a faith dependent upon signs (2:23-24; 3:2-3; 4:45-48; 6:14-15; 7:3-7). A key task of John's Gospel is to move people on from an inadequate level of faith, resting upon signs, to full Johannine faith. This mature faith "accompanies" the sign and penetrates to its deeper meaning. It sees the miracle, the remedying of an ordinary human need, as a *symbol* of a far greater reality connected with the presence of Jesus.

"Glory"

In connection with the presence of Jesus it will be helpful to say something about the link between the "signs" and "glory" in the Fourth Gospel. "Glory" (*doxa*) is an important concept for John. The appearance of the term has its origin in the Old Testament, where "glory" always has to do with the presence and power of God. In the biblical tradition God cannot be seen by human beings. But God's presence and power can be seen in the created world and felt in mighty saving acts. In the giving of the law on Sinai, God's "glory" was present in the thunder, lightning and other terrifying phenomena that issued from the mountain. Here, to encounter God's glory meant death for man and beast (Ex 19:9-25; 34:18-23, 29-35). The Israelites could not bear to look upon even the reflected glory of God remaining on the face of Moses; he had to promulgate the law wearing a veil lest even this reflection of God's glory bring harm to human beings (Ex 34:33-35).

The Fourth Gospel in its Prologue (1:1-18) clearly plays off the revelation of God's glory in Jesus against this Exodus-Sinai background. In contrast to the Israelites for whom the sight of God's glory meant death, who were even troubled by the reflected glory on Moses' face, the Johannine community asserts boldly: "And the Word became flesh and dwelt amongst us . . .; we have beheld his glory, glory as of the only Son from the Father" (v. 14). The divine glory, which in the old covenant remained in terrifying but necessary isolation on the mountain, has actually descended to earth in the person of Jesus. Where once it spelt death to see the glory of God, now to behold the glory in the flesh of Jesus is to find life. "No one has ever seen God" (v. 18a)—that remains true; but "the only Son, who is ever in the bosom of the Father, he has made him known" (v. 18b). To "see the glory" is to receive Jesus' life-giving revelation of the Father.

In John's Gospel it is the cross that supremely manifests the glory of God. Faithful to his Father's commission (19:30), Jesus gives his life for the life of the world. In so doing he renders the divinity transparent to human beings as essentially self-giving love (cf. 1 John 4:8). The signs that Jesus performs on his way to the final revelation are anticipatory revelations of this glory (cf. the comment after the first sign, 2:11). Each reveals some aspect of the divine communication of life through Jesus. Sometimes before the curtain rises on a dramatic or operatic performance to reveal the full "glory" of the set, the audiences catches glimpses of what is to be revealed through chinks or openings of the curtain caused perhaps by a draught of wind. In the Fourth Gospel the "signs" function somewhat in the same way: they are preliminary revelations of glory before the culminating "hour" of the cross.

"Eternal Life" present and to come

John's Gospel, as we have seen, offers "life" to believers on the basis of Jesus' revelation of God's glory. But a certain ambiguity hovers around this central idea of "life." It is important for our purpose to explore this concept against the background of early Christian eschatology.

The early Christian community shared with the Judaism of its time a firm belief in an imminent intervention of God which would offer rescue and salvation from the ills of the present age. The onset of this divine intervention would mark off a clear division between the present age, characterized by sinfulness, suffering and persecution, and the "age to come," where the faithful would live in God's presence in full and lasting enjoyment of the blessings of salvation. In this final age "life" for human beings would finally arrive at that richness intended by the Creator from the start.

In most forms of this eschatological hope certain human or, in some cases, quasi-angelic figures were expected to play a prominent role in the events leading up to the "end." So, on the basis of various scriptural allusions, there was in varying degrees expectation that Elijah would return to the world (Mal 4:5), that God would send a prophet "like Moses" (cf. Deut 18:15) or raise up a worthy high-priest and/or worthy king of David's line or, more vaguely, "the one who is to come." All would be "messianic" figures in the sense that they were understood in biblical categories as "anointed" by the Spirit for their eschatological task. In a particular way each would bear and communicate the life-giving gift of the Spirit. A crucial stage in the events leading up to the divine intervention would be the appearance, recognition and "installation" of one or several of these figures.

Among this complex of eschatological ideas was the hope

for a general resurrection of the dead. "Resurrection" was a device whereby the just who had died could be restored to life so as to share in the eschatological blessings. By this means the Israel of the end time would not lack its full complement of the deserving just.

These eschatological beliefs the early Christians shared with Jews of several tendencies. Only parties and sects of a strongly conservative stamp such as the Sadducees viewed such ideas with disfavor. In one key area, however, Christian eschatology diverged sharply from Jewish patterns. This divergence had to do with what might be called the "eschatological program." While for Jews generally the divine intervention remained an object of hope, Christian faith in Jesus as Messiah necessarily implied that it was already under way. Under way, yes but not complete. The completion of the divine intervention, including the final judgment and the resurrection of the just, had to await the public appearance (*parousia*) or return of Jesus as messianic king and eschatological judge.

So the early Christian community found themselves living in a curious "in-between" time not catered for in the Jewish eschatology. They still awaited the coming of the Messiah, at least in the sense of a glorious "return" to complete his messianic task. They still awaited the general resurrection of the dead, according to the conventional Jewish belief. The crucial difference was that they believed that at least in the sole case of Jesus resurrection had *already* occurred, a resurrection which impinged upon their own personal lives in Jesus' gift of the Spirit. The Fourth Gospel exploits this present aspect of resurrection in a unique way.

The curious "in-between" period between Jesus' resurrection and his return posed a problem for the early Christian communities. The various ways in which they coped with it have left their mark on virtually all the mature documents of the New Testament. As the years wore on and Jesus did not return in messianic glory, the sharpness that so marked the earlier expectation began to wane. Negatively, the problems presented by the undetermined waiting had to be met: coping with the death of members of the community, sustaining flagging hope in the face of suffering. Positively, there was the impulse to work out a theological rationale for the situation of the community in this period - the "time of the Church." So in the Gospels of Matthew and Luke and in the letter to the Ephesians, we find the Church itself becoming an object of theological reflection, with the "in-between" period of its life seen as an epoch in the history of salvation.

Towards the end of the New Testament era the Gospel of John made its own distinctive contribution to this theological task. It did so chiefly through its concept of an "eternal life" that was available here and now in the presence of Jesus. True, we find in John's Gospel clear traces of the more traditional eschatology, where judgment, resurrection and eternal life remain in the future:

> "Do not marvel at this, for the hour is coming
> when all who are in the tombs will hear his (the Son of Man's) voice and come forth,
> those who have done good, to the resurrection of life,
> and those who have done evil, to the resurrection of judgment" (5:28-29; cf. 6:39-40, 54; 12:25, 48).

To these may be added various references in chap. 14 to a future coming of Jesus (14:3, 18, 28). But along with these expressions of a future eschatology, sometimes almost side by side with them, we have the presentation of the eschatological events and gifts as present here and now:

> "For as the Father raises the dead and gives them life, so also the Son gives life to whom he will" (5:21).
> "Truly, truly, I say to you, he who hears my word and believes him who sent me, has eternal life; he does not come into judgment, but has passed from death to life" (5:24; cf. 3:36; 6:47).

This is the "realized eschatology" of the Fourth Gospel, its teaching that in the presence of Jesus the eschatological events —death, resurrection, judgment, eternal life—are brought forward to the present moment. Here and now in the decision for or against faith the central issue of eternal life is determined.

We have here a conscious and daring theological endeavor to confront the "between the times" aspect of Christian existence. The terminology, "eternal life," is traditional. But "eternal" is given a new meaning. Through the present gift of eternal life the believer comes to share already something of the eternal, death-defying existence of the risen Jesus. The gift of life in the distinctive Johannine sense has not simply to do with the life of the world to come. It implies also the transformation of present existence. It has to do with the supreme enhancement of life that accrues from the new understanding of oneself, one's world and God—all that is summed up in the Johannine concept of "truth." The aspect of a future hope that transcends the grave is not set aside. But "life" is redefined and death itself seen in a new way.[5]

Literary Techniques of the Fourth Gospel

a) Misunderstanding

Frequently throughout the Gospel those who hear Jesus or converse with him fail to grasp his proper meaning. More precisely, they take his statements at face value or in terms of their own unexamined needs or wishes and fail to realize that he is speaking about a totally different order of reality. Abundant illustration of this is provided by the figures of Nicodemus and the Samaritan Woman in chaps. 3 and 4 of the Gospel (3:3-4; 4:10-11, 14-15, 31-35). Such misunderstandings continue throughout the Gospel (6:34; 7:35-36; 8:21-22; 12:34). Through this literary device the evangelist constantly prods the reader to move towards the symbolic level on which alone Jesus' words can be grasped as revelation. Making the misunderstanding explicit effectively points up the gap between the commonplace, worldly interpretation of Jesus and the true inner meaning of his presence. To fully understand Jesus and what it is he has to offer one must pass from an ordinary view of life to a deeper reality of which the ordinary, even the miraculous provision of the ordinary, functions simply as a symbol.[6]

b) Irony

Closely associated with misunderstanding in the Fourth

Gospel is the use of irony. Irony occurs when characters are placed or place themselves in situation where, unbeknown to them, but known to the reader, there is a comic or tragic contrast between appearance and reality. In the Fourth Gospel the potential for irony is set up by the Prologue, which so impressively proclaims the origin and status of Jesus. From the start, then, the reader is "in the know" concerning his true identity as unique Son of God. The questionings and wrestlings of other characters about where Jesus comes from and where he is going (e.g.,1:46; 6:42; 7:35-36, 42) acquire, in the light of this knowledge, an ironical value that greatly increases the dramatic tension.

Above all, the Fourth Gospel employs irony to show how God's purpose works through and ultimately frustrates the best efforts of Jesus' adversaries to crush him. The supreme instance of this comes when the Jerusalem authorities realize they must take action to curb the growing influence of Jesus. Otherwise, they reason (11:48), "the Romans will come and destroy both our holy place and our nation." Every reader of the Gospel was well aware that by the time it had been written the Romans had done just what the leaders feared. Moreover, the High Priest's subsequent prophecy (v. 50) that it was expedient that "one man should die for the people" had an ironical fulfillment when Jesus' death on the cross had the effect of drawing a new people of God from all the world (12:32). In this way irony keeps the reader constantly in mind of the "real story," the divine purpose, running through the overt action.[7]

c) *Interplay of Sign and Discourse*

Even a surface glance reveals how much of the Fourth Gospel is taken up by lengthy speech or discourse on the part of Jesus. Most passages of this kind are related to the "signs" he performs. The discourse is often prompted by the "sign" and draws out the true, symbolic meaning of the miraculous event. We can see this clearly in the long discourses that follow the signs in both chap. 5 (the healing of the paralytic at the pool) and chap. 6 (the multiplication of the loaves and fishes). In chap. 9 the brief account of the coming to sight of the man born blind is followed by a long dramatic narrative which functions as a discourse about spiritual enlightenment and blindness. In other cases the simple "sign + discourse" sequence is altered. The two Cana miracles (2:1-11 and 4:46-54) both illustrate something about faith. Together, like bookends holding volumes upon a shelf, they "frame" a block of discourse material that is largely concerned with "correct" faith. In chap. 11, as we shall see, elements of discourse—notably the dialogue between Jesus and Martha—are woven into the narrative in such a way as to make plain the symbolic nature of the sign, which in this case concludes the whole drama. Throughout John's presentation of Jesus' public ministry (chaps. 2-12) a subtle and varied interplay of sign and discourse operates in this mutually illuminating way.

The "Lazarus" Sequence in the Structure of the Fourth Gospel

A major break in the Fourth Gospel clearly occurs at the close of chap. 12. The public revelation of Jesus, which began with the first "sign" given at Cana described in 2:1-11, concludes at this point with a summary statement referring to all the signs he had given (12:37-50). Chapters 2-12, then, constitute a complete whole, aptly called by C.H. Dodd, the "Book of Signs." Preceding this "Book of Signs" is the introductory part of the Gospel (chap. 1), consisting of the Prologue (1:1-18) and the testimony of John the Baptist (1:19-51).[8] At the conclusion of the Book of Signs the public revelation of Jesus to the world is complete: the light has shone in the darkness and for the most part the darkness has not received it. At the beginning of chap 13 there is a total change of direction and tone. Now, at the hands of those who have chosen the darkness, Jesus begins to make his journey to the Father (13:1-3). His true audience from now on is the select band of disciples. What we have, then, in chaps. 13-20 (chap. 21 forms an appendix to the first edition of the Gospel) is aptly named the "Book of Glory" or the "Book of Jesus' Return to the Father."

Within this basic division of the Gospel, the Lazarus episode occurs as the culmination of the "Book of Signs." At the same time it serves as a bridge to the "Book of Glory," more specifically to the account of the Passion. This is because the raising of Lazarus forms the "trigger" that sets off the process leading inevitably to Jesus' death. The narrative also pointedly raises the themes of life, death and resurrection. Thus, along with the associated material in chap. 12, it serves in many ways as the pivot upon which the whole action swings.

Let us now look for a moment more narrowly at the *preceding context* to chap. 11. At the beginning of chap. 7 Jesus on his own initiative leaves his native region, Galilee, and "goes up" to Jerusalem for the Feast of Tabernacles. The significance of this particular feast lies in the fact that it was at the joyous harvest festival of Tabernacles that, according to tradition, the Messiah was expected to appear. This is why Jesus' appearance in Jerusalem at Tabernacles raises acutely the question of messiahship with which the debates and dialogues of chaps. 7 and 8 are largely concerned.

Jesus does not deny he is the Messiah, but neither is he content to be grasped simply within Jewish messianic categories. These are completely inadequate to convey the fullness of his relationship to the Father. In mysterious allusions to his death he speaks of a revelation that will take place when they have "lifted up" the Son of Man: "When you have lifted up the Son of Man, then you will know that I am he" (8:28). This last phrase, "I am he" (literally "I am"), which occurs also at 8:24, 58; 13:19, has echoes of the revelation of God's name to Moses at the episode of the Burning Bush (Exod 3:14; cf. also Isa 41:4; 43:10, 13, 25; 45:18; 48:12; 51:12; 52:6). What will occur on the cross is not simply messianic exaltation ("the King of the Jews"), but a revelation of God's own being. Meanwhile the exchanges recorded in chaps. 7-8 bring out forcefully the hostility that now surrounds Jesus in Jerusalem: the sequence ends, in fact, with the the Jews attempting to stone him (8:50).

The Feast of Tabernacles also provides an appropriate background to the drama concerning the man born blind that follows in chap. 9. The theme of light arises naturally out of the feast since on the first night (and possibly on the others as well) the Temple was illuminated by torches. This custom lends added significance to Jesus' claim to be the "light of the world" (8:12; 9:5), a claim powerfully enacted in his bringing both physical and spiritual enlightenment to the man born blind.

Also central to the drama in John 9 is the contrast between the way in which the man is treated by the Jewish authorities and the care with which he is sought out and gently enlightened by Jesus. The sequence thus prefigures Jesus' claim in the subsequent chapter (10) to be the Good Shepherd (vv. 2, 11, 14), who knows his sheep, whose voice they recognize and follow.

It is in this context, too, that Jesus, as Good Shepherd, begins explicitly to speak of laying down his life for his sheep. He insists upon his sovereign freedom in this regard:

> "For this reason the Father loves me,
> because I lay down my life, that I may take it again.
> No one takes it from me, but I lay it down of my own accord. I have power to lay it down, and I have power to take it again;
> this charge I have received from my Father" (vv. 17-18).

It is important to keep this solemn statement in mind as we read chap. 11.

A further feast, the Dedication, provides the background to the discourse in the second half of chap. 10 (cf. v. 22). Dedication celebrated the purification and reconstitution of the Temple under the Maccabees. It also recalled the consecration of all the houses of God (Exodus tabernacle, Temple of Solomon, Temple of Ezra) in the tradition of Israel. Continuing the theme of "replacement" of Jewish institutions and feasts, Jesus here presents himself as the one "whom the Father has consecrated and sent into the world" (v. 36). Behind the sovereign personal freedom of Jesus and integrally woven into it is the divine appointment and mission. Jesus lays down his life for his sheep, he gives his life that they may have life, all as part of God's design to give life to the world.

So we approach the story of the raising of Lazarus in chap. 11 armed with this rich sequence in which Jesus is Light, Shepherd and Temple consecrated by the Father. All are connected with the theme of giving life. The last two especially emphasize that it will be through his self-giving in death that life will flow to the sheep.

Immediately *following* the episode of the raising of Lazarus the Gospel records the plot of the Jewish authorities to do away with Jesus (11:47-53). The stupendous public conquest of death is the "last straw" as far as they are concerned. If they do not act now, his influence with the people will become irreversible and from that they can see only ruin for the whole nation. So, as the High Priest puts it with prophetic irony as we have seen "it is expedient for you that one man should die for the people" (v. 50).

With Jesus' death now clearly decided in the public sphere, the action shifts once again to the circle of his own disciples. Mary, the sister of Lazarus, anoints the feet of Jesus with very precious ointment (12:1-8). Jesus defends her action on the grounds that it anticipates the anointing at his burial. Anointed in this way, Jesus makes his solemn messianic entry into the Holy City (12:12-19). Twice we are reminded during this incident that it is the raising of Lazarus that has excited the high interest and enthusiasm of the crowd (vv. 9, 17). So much so that the authorities have decided that Lazarus also must be put to death (vv. 10-11). In this way the evangelist continues to remind us of the intimate link between the raising of Lazarus and the inexorable movement towards Jesus' own death.

The remainder of chap. 12 is entirely taken up with Jesus' reflections and reactions as his "hour" approaches. The arrival of the Greeks and their desire to see him (vv. 20-22) sparks off his sense that the final crisis is at hand. Jesus knows that it is when he is lifted up from the earth (v. 32) that "all" (that is, including the Gentiles) will be drawn to himself. That is why the interest of the Greeks heralds the imminence of his "hour" and draws from him a moment of shrinking before the cost it will involve: "Father, save me from this hour" (v. 27). After a concluding reflection from the evangelist (vv. 37-43), the way lies open for the "Book of Glory" to begin, the account of the passion, death and risen life of Jesus as he makes his return to the Father (chaps. 13-20). In the whole sequence the raising of Lazarus marks the cresting of the wave that engulfs Jesus, leading to his death but also to his glory as the instrument of the Father to give life to the world.

2

The Structure and Literary Form of John 11:1-46

We have considered the wider context surrounding the story of Lazarus in John 11. We now turn our attention to the actual account itself. Before entering upon the details, however, there are some general questions to be resolved. These concern principally the structure and literary form of the narrative. What do we have in John 11:1-46?

Structure

John 11 divides fairly simply into a sequence of seven scenes. 1. Vv. 1-4 set the scene and the situation: a certain man, Lazarus, lies ill at Bethany, the village of Mary and Martha. Jesus is "across the Jordan," at the place where John had baptized. He receives the message: "he whom you love is ill" (v. 3) and states his first reaction (v. 4).

2. The second scene (vv. 5-16) occurs at the same location. It consists principally of a two-part deliberation between Jesus and his disciples about the perils and the motives for journeying to Judea in response to the sisters' request. Initially (vv. 5-6) we are reminded of Jesus' love for all three members of this family and given the surprising information that he delays two days before making any move. Jesus then proposes going to Judea and justifies this over the disciples' protest by means of

a parable about walking in the light of day, rather than in the night (vv. 7-10). In the second part of the deliberation (vv. 11-15) Jesus announces the death of Lazarus. He does so at first metaphorically, using the image of sleep. Then, following the disciples' misunderstanding, he tells them plainly that Lazarus is dead, insisting, paradoxically, that this is a cause of gladness, since it will enhance faith. Finally, the pessimistic but resigned Thomas voices the general agreement to go along with Jesus' plan (v. 16).

3. The action now moves to the vicinity of Bethany. A small bridge scene (vv. 17-19) tells us of Jesus' arrival and also informs us of the closeness of Bethany to Jerusalem. This vicinity has enabled many of the Jews to be present to offer sympathy.

The two central scenes of the episode comprise a meeting and exchange between Jesus and the two sisters, Martha and Mary.

4. In the first (vv. 20-27) Martha goes out to meet Jesus (v. 20). In gentle remonstration she suggests that, had he been present, her brother would not have died, but expresses, too, a vague confidence that even now God would hear his prayer (vv. 21-22). Jesus assures her that her brother will rise, but she understands his ambiguous assurance solely in terms of the conventional hope for general resurrection on the last day (vv. 23-24). At this point Jesus makes the climactic revelation of himself as the resurrection and the life (vv. 25-26ab). The scene ends with Martha expressing her faith in Jesus in terms of three messianic titles (vv. 26c-27).

5. The scene with Mary (vv. 28-32) begins as Martha returns to the house and calls her sister (v. 28). Mary goes out to Jesus (v. 29), followed by the Jewish mourners, who do not know her real intentions (vv. 30-31). She falls at his feet and makes the same remonstrance as her sister, though without the additional act of confidence (v. 32).

6. The encounter with Mary gives way to the events leading up to and including the raising itself (vv. 33-44). First, in the context of general distress on the part of Mary and the Jewish crowd (now arrived in the presence of Jesus) we are told at length of the emotions of Jesus himself (vv. 33-35) and of the

varying reactions of the crowd to this (vv. 36-37). When finally the scene shifts to the tomb itself (v. 38), there is a further exchange with Martha, who is reluctant to remove the stone (vv. 39-41a). A prayer of Jesus to the Father (vv. 41b-42) precedes the actual raising itself (vv. 43-44).

7. Finally, the reaction of the Jewish observers to the whole episode is recorded. Some believe in Jesus on the basis of the sign (v. 45). But others go and inform the Pharisees of the whole affair (v. 46), so setting in motion the plot that will lead inexorably to Jesus' own death.

We can set out this structure more schematically as follows:

1. The Situation: Lazarus ill; the message sent to Jesus; his initial reaction (vv. 1-4)

2. The Deliberation with the disciples: to Judea or not? (vv. 5-16)
　　Introduction: the two-day delay of Jesus (vv. 5-6)
　a) Walking in the Light (vv. 7-10)
　b) Lazarus "asleep" (vv. 11-15)
　　Conclusion: "Let us also go (Thomas) ..." (v. 16).

3. Bridge passage: Jesus' arrival at Bethany; the scene there (vv. 17-19)

4. Jesus and Martha (vv. 20-27)
　a) The meeting (v. 20)
　b) Martha's remonstrance and initial act of faith (vv. 21-22)
　c) Jesus' reassurance and Martha's conventional hope (vv. 23-24)
　d) Jesus' word of revelation: "I am the resurrection ..." (vv. 25-26ab)
　e) Martha's final act of faith (vv 26c-27).

5. Jesus and Mary (vv. 28-32)
　a) The summons and response of Mary (vv. 28-30)
　b) The misunderstanding and following of the Jews (v. 31)
　c) Mary's obeisance and remonstrance before Jesus (v. 32).

6. The Raising of Lazarus (vv. 33-44)
　a) The emotional reactions of Jesus (vv. 33-35)
　b) Reaction of the Jews (vv. 36-37)

c) The journey to the tomb (v. 38)
d) At the tomb: the hesitation and opening (vv. 39-41a)
e) The prayer of Jesus to his Father (vv. 41b-42)
f) The raising (vv. 43-44).

7. Reaction to the raising (vv. 45-46)
a) Positive (v. 45)
b) Negative: the event reported to the authorities (v. 46).

An outline such as this makes it clear that the exchanges between Jesus and the two sisters form the central core of the drama. The two exchanges stand in parallel, yet the one with Martha is far more developed in terms of both drama and theology. The revelation word of Jesus ("I am the resurrection and the life, . . . ," vv. 25-26) is the chief theological climax not only of the scene with Martha but of the entire episode. Alongside this, the exchange with Mary is at first sight a pale shadow. Closer inspection, however, reveals that this latter scene flows readily into the following sequence (section 6 of our structural analysis), which comes to a climax in the actual raising. The stress upon emotional reaction in the scene with Mary (section 5) continues as the narrative highlights the reactions of the Jews and of Jesus himself preceding the movement to the tomb.

So there is a sense in which the central core of the passage can be divided into two parts:
1. A meeting between Jesus and Martha, culminating in Jesus' word of revelation (vv. 20-27)
2. A meeting between Jesus and Mary, culminating in the miraculous raising of Lazarus from the tomb (vv. 28-44).

Such a division highlights a certain tension in the passage between what might be termed the theological and the dramatic climaxes. Clearly, the dramatic climax is reached only with the summons and emergence of Lazarus from the tomb. But in theological terms nothing can surpass the earlier self-revelation of Jesus to Martha as "resurrection and life."

It is in fact likely that the tension between the two possible points of climax is fully intended by the evangelist: the actual raising of Lazarus symbolically enacts the promise contained in the word of revelation. The miracle follows as a confirmatory sign of the exalted claim made earlier on. Here we have no anomaly but the supreme instance of the evangelist's skill in weaving theology and drama together in inventive and effective ways.[1]

The Literary Form of John 11:1-46

Central to the discovery of the meaning of a text is some determination of its literary form. When we pick up a newspaper we find information and entertainment cast in quite a variety of forms: editorials, news reports, feature articles, letters to the editor, sports pages, comic strips. Instinctively we adjust our understanding to this variety. We do not look to the editorials for detailed information about events. We know we are not to take the sports headlines—"Saints maul Tigers," for example—literally. We read all these elements in a way appropriate to their particular literary form or genre.

It is generally accepted today that this consideration applies equally to biblical texts and in particular to the gospels. In our examination of the Lazarus episode in John 11 we must ask whether we are dealing with a specific literary genre and, if this proves to be the case, interpret it in the way appropriate for such a genre.

The discovery and identification of genre proceeds chiefly from examining material of similar content and structure and seeing whether distinct common patterns emerge. If such a pattern can be found we can be fairly confident that the author is not simply describing an incident as an eye-witness might testify to an accident or some other happening. Rather, like the writer of a letter or a poem, the author is communicating with us according to a set conventional form which sets up a pattern of shared assumption and expectation. To enquire, then, about the literary form of John 11 is chiefly to ask whether there are other episodes in the biblical tradition with which it may profitably be compared.

Biblical Accounts of Raising: Old and New Testament

John 11:1-46 is fundamentally a miracle story and a miracle

story of a particularly distinctive kind: the account of the raising of a dead person. The biblical tradition contains several such accounts. In the Old Testament miracles of raising are attributed to two prophets. Elijah raises the son of the widow of Sarephta (1 Kings 17:17-24); his protégé Elisha raises the son of the woman from Shunem (2 Kings 4:18-37; there is a résumé of this episode in 2 Kings 8:4-6). The two accounts stand in close parallel: in both cases the dead person is the son of a woman previously favored by the prophet; the prophet shuts himself up with the dead boy in an enclosed room and prays; the boy revives and is given back to the mother, who recognizes the authority of the prophet. In the New Testament, apart from John 11, four incidents are recorded which involve the raising of a person believed to be dead. In Luke 7:11-17 Jesus raises the son of the widow of Nain; in Mark 5:21-43 (parallel Matt 9:18-26; Luke 8:40-56) he raises the daughter of Jairus. In Acts 9:36-42 Peter raises Tabitha; in Acts 20:7-12 Paul revives the young man who had fallen, apparently to his death, from an upper-storey window. The incident at Nain has many affinities with the account of Elijah's raising in 1 Kings 17 and the same can be said of the raising of Tabitha in Acts 9. Clearly, the activity of the Old Testament prophets has established a pattern upon which both accounts are based.[2]

With this whole tradition the Lazarus miracle in John 11 has very little in common. In John 11, as in the Old Testament stories, Jesus responds, as do the prophets, to the pleas of a relative of the deceased. He prays, as they do, before the actual raising, but has no need of the gestures of revival (stretching upon the body and so forth). Moreover, the demand for faith, so central in John 11, is quite lacking in the Old Testament accounts and even in that of Luke 7. With all these the Lazarus episode, in its present form, has very little similarity.

The raising of the daughter of Jairus (Mark 5:21-43 and parallels) presents points of closer contact. As in the case of Lazarus, the first report is that the child is grievously ill. Jesus proceeds at once, but then comes the long "interruption" while attention is given to the woman with a haemorrhage (vv. 25-34). Then comes the second report: the child has in fact died. This becomes for Jesus an occasion to insist upon persevering faith (vv. 35-36). Here we have something correspon-

ding to the "delay" of Jesus in John 11, in the course of which
Lazarus dies. Another point of contact lies in the context of
demonstrative grief—weeping and wailing—provided by the
bystanders. In both incidents this provokes strong reaction in
Jesus, who in Mark 5 (v. 39), as in John 11, describes the state
of the dead person as "sleep." Like Lazarus (and also the son
of the widow of Nain) the little girl is summoned back to life
by the simple command of Jesus.

All these points of contact, however, do little to compensate
for the substantial differences between the Johannine sign and
these other biblical instances of raising the dead. In its far
greater dramatic and theological development, in its linking of
the miracle with the proclamation of Jesus as himself "the
resurrection and the life," in the heightening of the miraculous
by having Jesus raise a person four days dead: in all these
ways the Lazarus episode in its present form completely outstrips the comparable biblical tradition. Perhaps at an earlier
stage of its composition (which we shall consider later) the
tradition behind John 11 did stand in rather greater similarity
to the synoptic raisings. All such accounts cohere in being
principally dramatic illustrations that in Jesus' presence there
has dawned the messianic hope of resurrection. But the
Lazarus episode in its present form so greatly enlarges upon
the earlier patterns in dramatic and theological terms that it is
hard to justify its association with them in any set literary
form. We shall return to these other raising traditions when
considering the history behind the composition of John 11.

The Johannine Signs

So unique in this sense is the raising story in John 11 that in
seeking a literary/theological form against which to compare
it we are really forced back to the other "signs" of the Fourth
Gospel. We have already discussed the signs in general, noting
in particular the pattern into which they fall, their association
with levels of faith and the revelation of God's glory in Jesus.
The raising of Lazarus exhibits all these features of a "sign,"
save only that, unlike the signs in John 5, 6 and 9, the actual
miracle comes at the end rather than the beginning of the
dramatic sequence.

What the raising of Lazarus has in common with all other Johannine signs is the essential point whereby a miraculous event becomes for faith a symbol of a deeper and more pervasive revelation. There are, however, several further points of contact. The two-day delay of Jesus, after receiving the sisters' desperate message, corresponds to the initial rebuff given to his mother at the wedding feast of Cana (2:4) and to a similar challenge to the royal steward (4:48) at the same village (cf. also his refusal to "go up for the feast" [Tabernacles] at the urging of his brothers [7:6-9]). Human need, human request does not control the Johannine Jesus. He acts upon his own divine agenda, which to mature, persevering faith discloses the life-giving revelation. At a culminating point in the discourse of John 6 Jesus exclaims "I am the bread of life" (v. 35; cf vv. 41, 51) in much the same way as he reveals himself to be the "resurrection and the life' in John 11. With this we may compare the claim to be the "light of the world" in the healing of the man born blind (chap. 9; cf. v. 5). Indeed it is with these last two, immediately preceding signs that the sign recounted in chap. 11 has most in common.

Nonetheless, the differences in dramatic structure are so great that we can hardly speak of a distinctive literary from covering all the Johannine signs. What we have is a distinctive technique whereby, with considerable freedom, the evangelist points to a situation of human need, describes how Jesus responds to the need miraculously and then, by means of discourse and dramatic structure, shows how the miracle acts as symbol of a deeper revelation: the revelation of Jesus as life-giving emissary of the Father.

3

The Raising of Lazarus: Detailed Commentary on John 11:1-46

We are now in a position to examine the text of John 11:1-46 more closely. While attending to detail, we shall also endeavor to keep the larger picture in mind, especially the structure of the passage just outlined. The aim all through will be to build up a coherent understanding of the whole sequence.

1. Vv. 1-4: Lazarus is ill; a message is sent to Jesus; his initial reaction.

V. 1: *Now a certain man was ill, Lazarus of Bethany, the village of Mary and her sister Martha.*

This opening sentence introduces the chief characters of the drama and indicates the situation of human need (grave illness) which the sign will address. It is not immediately clear from this verse that Lazarus is in fact the brother of the two sisters Mary and Martha; he could simply be a person from the same village. Nor does the all-important factor of Jesus' personal love for him emerge till later on (vv. 3, 6). As it stands the sentence seems to imply that it is Mary who is the chief link with Jesus, though in the subsequent drama she will play a lesser role than her sister.

Taken in isolation, this opening sentence corresponds rather well to the situation presupposed in Luke 10:38-42. Two sisters, Martha and Mary, entertain Jesus in the course of his journey to Jerusalem; one of them, Mary, to the displeasure of her sister, adopts a position of closer intimacy with Jesus. The Lucan story makes no mention of a brother, Lazarus, and leaves unnamed the village where the episode occurred. But both gospels seem to be drawing upon a common early tradition, reflected more accurately in this opening sentence of John 11 than in the subsequent drama. How the various traditions underlying the narrative relate to one another is a question I propose to take up later on. For the present it is probably safe to propose that it was the evangelist who bound the three characters into one family by making Lazarus the brother of Mary and Martha (cf. v. 21, v. 32, v. 39).

The evangelist was also happy to locate the scene in Bethany, a village about two miles distant from Jerusalem on the eastern side of the Mount of Olives. In the wider action of the Fourth Gospel the significance of Bethany lies, of course, in its proximity to Jerusalem: the city of threat for Jesus (5:18; 7:1, 19, 25, 30, 44; 8:20, 37, 59; 10:31, 39). If Jesus leaves the safe country ("across the Jordan," 10:40) where he is when the message reaches him and ventures as close to the capital as Bethany, he places his own life in mortal danger.

V. 2: *It was Mary who anointed the Lord with ointment and wiped his feet with her hair, whose brother Lazarus was ill.*

This statement has commonly been regarded as an explanatory gloss added by a later editor to identify this particular Mary amongst the several bearers of the name associated with Jesus. The rather curious reference to an event yet to come (12:1-8) as though it had already taken place and other un-Johannine features (such as the reference to Jesus as "the Lord") lends some plausibility to this view. But, to take the text as it now stands, the identification plays an important role in the whole sequence. Right from the start it ties the event about to be described, the death and raising of Lazarus, to the death of Jesus, since Mary's anointing is later explicitly interpreted as a preparation for burial (12:7).

Also, in a context stressing Jesus' love for members of this family, mention of Mary's act of loving devotion reminds us that the family reciprocated that love. Later, in the actual account of the anointing, we are told that Martha was serving and Lazarus was one of those at table (12:2). What Jesus will do for Lazarus, then, takes place in a context of mutual love and affection, cemented in table fellowship. This will be of significance when later we raise the question as to what extent Lazarus serves as a type or representative of every believer, beloved of Jesus.

V. 3: *So the sisters sent to him, saying, "Lord, he whom you love is ill."*

Implicit in the sisters' message is a request for Jesus to come or at least do something about the situation.[1] The message contains the first of several allusions to Jesus' love for Lazarus. Referring to their brother in such terms, without mention of his name, the sisters concentrate attention upon the one thing which distinguishes him: that he is loved by Jesus. Lazarus is to be totally passive in this story; we are to learn nothing of his character, virtue or worth in any way (contrast the clear characterization of the man born blind in John 9). His role is simply to be the one loved by Jesus.

V. 4: *But when Jesus heard it he said, "This illness is not unto death; it is for the glory of God, so that the Son of God may be glorified by means of it."*

In Jesus' reaction on receiving the message from Bethany we hear a note that is unmistakably Johannine. The statement that Lazarus' illness is not unto death is ambiguous—and deliberately so—on several levels. At simple face value Jesus' response could be taken by the disciples to mean that Lazarus' illness will not be fatal. In this sense, however, it is not true: the sickness *is* "unto death" because Lazarus is shortly going to die. It is "unto death" in a further sense because through raising the man killed by this illness Jesus will set in motion the events leading to his own death. In neither case, however, is the illness *ultimately* "unto death," since Lazarus will be brought back to ordinary human life and Jesus himself will rise to a totally new order of existence.

But the conquest of death is not tied solely to the resurrection. In this gospel, as we have seen, when Jesus speaks of his "glorification" the reference includes his death upon the cross (cf. esp. 12:16, 23, 28; 13:31-32; 17:1, 4-5) since it is in that event that his oneness with the Father, his "transparency" to the Godhead, is most apparent. Jesus' death is the high point of glory, the revelation to believers of God's life-giving power and presence in the world.

So in two senses this illness of Lazarus "is for the glory of God." Firstly, like the affliction of the man born blind (cf. 9:3b), it will occasion a sign of Jesus - and, as we have noted above, signs are in this gospel anticipatory glimpses of the glory of Jesus. Secondly and more importantly, it is for the glory of God in the sense that it will trigger the process leading to Jesus' own death, an event which will supremely constitute the life-giving revelation of God's glory to human beings. As Jesus said to Nicodemus, alluding to the serpent lifted up by Moses in the wilderness, "..., so must the Son of Man be lifted up, that whoever believes in him may have eternal life" (3:14-15). Since the death of Jesus is ultimately for the life of the world, the illness of Lazarus which remotely brings it about is not a sickness "unto death." On the contrary, it is supremely "unto life." The title "Son of God" occurs in the gospel particularly in contexts where Jesus presents himself as one with the Father in giving life (3:16-18; 5:19-29; 10:36).

2. Vv. 5-16: The Deliberation with the Disciples: to Judea or not?

The second scene is basically taken up with a dialogue between Jesus and his disciples as to whether they should go to Lazarus or not. The role of the disciples in the narrative begins and ends with this deliberation. They function simply as dialogue partners of Jesus, their objections and misunder-standings serving to bring out both the danger of Jesus' pro-posal and its inner motivation. Behind the deliberation is the abiding presupposition that Judea (including Jerusalem and its surrounding villages, such as Bethany) is a place of mortal danger (see esp. v. 8, v. 16). In the face of this fact everything is designed to show how fateful and deliberate is the decision Jesus makes to go and bring life to Lazarus.

Vv. 5-6. Introduction: the two-day delay:
V. 5. *Now Jesus loved Martha and her sister and Lazarus.*

To set up the dramatic tension surrounding the deliberation of Jesus, the evangelist reminds us once more of Jesus' love for this family. We knew already of his love for Lazarus (v. 3). We are now told of his affection for Martha and her sister as well. This is significant because from the start it suggests that the concern and action of Jesus is addressed as much to the grief of the sisters as it is to the plight of Lazarus himself. The sign he will eventually perform will not simply constitute a remedy for death. It will address also the human grieving for death, represented here by the sisters.

We have also in v. 5 a first indication of Martha's prominence in the story. She is mentioned first and by name; Mary is simply "her sister" and Lazarus, surprisingly, comes third. Aside from Jesus himself, the fine point of focus will rest upon Martha—in particular upon her wrestling with faith and grief.

V. 6. *So when he heard that he was ill, he stayed two days longer in the place where he was.*

On hearing the sisters' message, Jesus stays two days longer where he was. Following upon the remark about Jesus' love in the preceding sentence, the delay comes as a severe surprise. It is not the response of a friend. The evangelist, moreover, heightens the conflict by prefacing the second statement with "so," "therefore" (Greek *oun*). The juxtaposition of the statements in vv. 5 and 6 sets up the contrast very starkly. Jesus loves . . . , yet Jesus stays. In effect, as will become apparent, Jesus lets Lazarus die. How is this compatible with love? Twice this inconsistency will be put before us again—in the remonstrances uttered by each of the sisters in turn on meeting Jesus: "Lord, if you had been here, my brother would not have died" (vv. 21, 32). Something very central to the whole episode is being held before us here: the incompatibility—or compatibility—between (God's) love and (God's) letting people die.[2]

Jesus' delaying two days after receiving the message about Lazarus follows a pattern that can be seen elsewhere in this gospel. In the first Cana miracle he brushes off the request implicit in his mother's observation about the lack of wine (2:4). In the second Cana miracle he does not accede to the royal official's request to come down and attend to his son; he issues instead what is virtually an accusation about the inadequacy of his faith (4:48). When there is question of his going up to the feast of Tabernacles, Jesus will not move at the urging of his brethren; he goes up privately somewhat later (7:2-10). Human agenda, human need—no matter how desperate—does not control the Johannine Jesus. He has his own divine timetable and will not be imprisoned in any other. To give in simply to human demand would be to promote an inferior faith, one wrapped up in its own needs, wholly inadequate to discern and receive the life-giving revelation. Full, radical faith must await and come to recognize the divine agenda to which alone Jesus responds. On a more matter-of-fact level, the two-day delay allows for the four days during which, according the narrative (v. 39), Lazarus has been in his tomb when Jesus and the disciples finally arrive.

a) Vv. 7-10: Walking in the Light.

Vv. 7-8: [7] *Then after this he said to the disciples, "Let us go into Judea again."* [8] *The disciples said to him, "Rabbi, the Jews were but now seeking to stone you, and are you going there again?"*

The deliberation commences with Jesus' proposal in v. 7 and concludes, in a way that forms a literary "inclusion," with Thomas' resigned and pessimistic echoing of it in v. 16. The proposal is to go "into Judea," rather than specifically to the village of Lazarus. The use of the wider geographical term highlights the danger that attends the plan.

The response of the disciples (v. 8) makes this point quite plainly. They recall that in his recent appearances in Jerusalem Jesus has narrowly escaped death by stoning on at least two occasions (8:59; 10:31). There is good reason to suppose that a further visit will encounter similar hostility. The phrase "the Jews" here has the technical, non-ethnic sense normally prevailing in the Fourth Gospel, designating all who become through personal choice the adversaries of Jesus. Elsewhere in this chapter, however, the phrase has a somewhat more benign reference. "The Jews" are inhabitants of Jerusalem who come out to Bethany to console the two sisters. In the end, of course, some will perform the negative act of reporting Jesus to the authorities (v. 46).

Vv. 9-10: The Parable:

> *Jesus answered, "Are there not twelve hours in the day?*
>
> | *If any one walks in the day,* | [A] |
> | *he does not stumble,* | [B] |
> | *because he sees the light of this world.* | [C] |
> | *But if he walks in the night,* | [A'] |
> | *he stumbles,* | [B'] |
> | *because the light is not in him.* | [C'] |

Jesus' response to the hesitation of the disciples comes in the form of a parable. The parable consists of a rhetorical question followed by two balanced sentences, each consisting of three clauses, standing in antithetical parallelism. It presupposes awareness both of Jewish ways of telling time in Jesus' day and also a distinctive understanding of light. The day was reckoned from sunrise to sunset and divided into twelve hours (which meant, of course, that the length of an "hour" varied depending on the time of the year). The day, then, was strictly the time during which one could see. What gave the ability to see was the light of the sun which created light "in" the eye. Absence of light (from the sun) without meant an absence of light within. Thus not "having the light" (cf. 12:35-36) meant failure to see.

As is typical of imagery in the Fourth Gospel, the parable shows several layers of meaning. At the most basic, everyday level the point would be that since Jesus' final hour has not yet come he—and the disciples—can walk in safety without fear of harm from his adversaries; they can go to Judea and attend to Lazarus as if walking in the safety of the day, lit up by the "light of the world", that is, the sun.

At the same time, one can hardly read this parable without thinking of Jesus' similar statement when his attention falls upon the condition of the man born blind: "We must work the works of him who sent me, while it is day; night comes, when no one can work. As long as I am in the world, I am the light of the world" (9:4-5). Read as a commentary on the parable in John 11, this suggests that the idea of a limit upon Jesus' activity is also at hand: Jesus must go and give life to Lazarus because the time is coming (the darkness) when such activity will no longer be possible. We can indeed hold both ideas together: because it is still "day", Jesus *can* go in safety to Lazarus and he must go *now* since time is running out. But perhaps we should not allow the parallel from John 9:4-5 to swamp the primary meaning of the parable in the present context. Jesus allays the disciples' fears by assuring them that the time of his mortal danger is still to come: there are twelve hours in the day and the last is not yet at hand.

At a deeper level, however, it is difficult to hear this parable without recalling that constantly in this gospel the "light of the world" is Jesus himself (1:4; 8:12; 9:5; 12:46). Within this christological understanding the clause "because the light is not in him" (v. 10c) must refer to the lack of inner light within a disciple who no longer walks with Jesus. At this level the parable becomes an exhortation to the disciples not to be afraid to go with Jesus to Judea. Since they will be with him, the Light, they will always be walking by day no matter how threatening the night of opposition. If they choose not to walk with him, no matter how secure they may feel in their "safe territory," they will be choosing the darkness. The thought is then very close to that of 12:35: ". . . .The light is with you for a little longer. Walk while you have the light, lest the darkness overtake you; he who walks in the darkness does not know where he goes."

b) Vv. 11-15: Lazarus "asleep":

V. 11: *Thus he spoke, and then he said to them, "Our friend Lazarus has fallen asleep, but I go to awake him out of sleep."*

We move now into the second part of the deliberation between Jesus and his disciples. The opening, rather overloaded phrase, "Thus he spoke, and then he said to them," may at one level betray the editorial hand of the evangelist. On the other hand, it suggests perhaps a pause, a space for reflection upon the exhortation implicit in the parable before moving on. Then Jesus renews his proposal of going to Lazarus, using the image of "sleep," around which this whole development will revolve.

This way of speaking about death was common parlance in the early Christian community. We find it in the Pauline writings—for example, 1 Thess 4:13-14; 1 Cor 15:6,18, 20, 51. Again, in the synoptic account of the raising of the daughter of Jairus, Jesus, in the face of all the weeping and wailing of the mourners, insists that the child is not dead but "asleep" (Matt 13:24; Mark 5:39; Luke 8:52). Through such language the community expressed its hope of resurrection. As sleep is a condition from which one wakes refreshed and renewed, so for believers death is only a temporary absence, a prelude to risen life.

On Jesus' lips here in John 11 this talk of "sleep" probably goes beyond the standard Christian metaphor. Already the discerning reader, who knows what Jesus purposes to do, may pick up the deeper meaning in "I go to wake him." It is not a matter simply of Lazarus "waking" at the general resurrection. Jesus is going to anticipate that event by "waking" him here and now. In this sense the disciples' mistaken assumption, "he will recover" (lit. "he will be saved") ironically speaks the truth. Lazarus will find salvation, but only because Jesus goes to raise him.

Vv. 12-13: [12]*The disciples said to him, "Lord, if he has fallen asleep, he will recover."* [13]*Now Jesus had spoken of his death, but they thought that he meant taking rest in sleep.*

We meet here a classic instance of the Johannine technique of misunderstanding. Jesus' language of "sleep" and "waking" is ambiguous. As v. 13 explains to us, the disciples think he is speaking about ordinary sleep. With evident relief they seize upon this information: if Lazarus is sleeping common wisdom in the matter of health suggests he will recover; the dangerous proposal of journeying to Judea can now be safely set aside. But this is a blind alley. Jesus is speaking of the "sleep" of death" and "waking" Lazarus means resurrection.

The disciples' misunderstanding will give Jesus the chance to clarify his original statement and so bring out explicitly and dramatically the deeper levels of meaning. A fearful, hesitant following of Jesus, such as the disciples now illustrate, anchors a person on a level that misses the point completely. Even the basic Christian sense of death as a "sleep" in the hope of resurrection is going to be proved inadequate in the end. The present decisive proposal to go and "wake" Lazarus from his sleep already presages the startling claim Jesus is soon to make: to be here and now "the resurrection and the life" (v. 25).

Vv. 14-15: [14]*Then Jesus told them plainly, "Lazarus is dead;* [15]*and for your sake I am glad that I was not there, so that you may believe. But let us go to him."*

Faced with the misunderstanding of the disciples, Jesus declares the plain fact bluntly: "Lazarus is dead." The quasi theological language of "sleeping," a palliative to the sharp pang of death, is here almost brutally brushed aside. Addressed as it is to the problem of death in the community of believers, the entire sequence proposes no remedy that seeks to turn aside or cover over the harsh fact of death. Lazarus is dead— as believers have died and will die. Whatever remedy Jesus brings to death confronts the reality head on. There is no denial of death, no message of pious, glib comfort here.

Jesus goes even further. Provocatively he states (v. 15) that he is "glad" he was not there. This is because, as both sisters will later suggest, his presence would have prevented Lazarus from dying. He is glad he was not there because the death of Lazarus will present the disciples with a chance to "believe," to come to deeper faith.[3] The reality of death is both the supreme challenge to faith and the greatest spur for its exercise. Of the disciples and their faith we will, in fact, hear no more. It is Martha—and through her the subsequent Christian believer— whom Jesus will challenge to work through this death to a deeper level of faith.

V.16: *Thomas, called the Twin, said to his fellow disciples, "Let us also go, that we may die with him."*

The deliberation ends with a resigned, pessimistic acceptance by Thomas of Jesus' proposal to go to Judea. That such a pessimistic appraisal of the likely future should come from Thomas is of a piece with what little emerges of his character in the rest of the gospel (cf.14:5; 20:25). He is the realist who understands well enough that to follow Jesus means risking death. His statement underlines once again the fact that Jesus is putting his own life in mortal danger by going to Judea. At the same time, by not seeing anything but death in the proposal, Thomas continues the earlier misunderstanding of the disciples. He has no sense of the deeper meaning: that Jesus' death will also be his exaltation, his return to the Father in glory (cf. 14:5). His attitude illustrates how sharply in Johannine terms faith moves away from fixation upon earthly realities alone.[4]

3. Bridge Passage: Vv. 17-19:
Jesus' arrival at Bethany; the scene there.

V. 17: *Now when Jesus came, he found that Lazarus had already been in the tomb four days.*

The scene now shifts to the neighborhood of Bethany. From what follows it appears that Jesus neither goes directly to the house of Martha and Mary nor to the tomb. His "finding" then "that Lazarus had already been four days in the tomb" presupposes some message that meets him on the way. The language of "finding," however, may have deeper meaning. Jesus "finds" the tomb of Lazarus occupied. The disciples are going to find *his* tomb empty (20:1-10). Already we seem to have a contrasting parallel being set up between the raising of Lazarus and the rising of Jesus.

Lazarus, however, has "already been in the tomb four days." In contemporary belief the soul of the deceased hovered about the corpse for some time after death. By the fourth day, however, the features of the deceased were no longer recognizable. This was taken to be a sign that the soul had definitively left the corpse and irreversible corruption set in.[5] If Lazarus, then, is four days dead, the miracle required to raise him will be a stupendous one indeed, going well beyond the limits of any other biblical raising. At the same time, precisely because he has been subject not simply to death but also to corruption, Lazarus achieves a wider significance. In his death and four-day entombment he can represent all who undergo the normal processes of death and corruption. His raising, then, will not be simply an exceptional case of temporary respite from death. It will be a symbol, a pledge of something offered to all.

Vv. 18-19: [18] *Bethany was near Jerusalem, about two miles off,* [19] *and many of the Jews had come to Martha and Mary to console them concerning their brother.*

The evangelist gives us (v. 18) geographical information about the locality. His motivation, however, is primarily theological. He wants to make sure we are aware of the proximity of Bethany to Jerusalem, the city of threat to Jesus.

The closeness to the capital also allows for the presence of "many of the Jews" (v. 19). As noted above, "the Jews" are inhabitants of Jerusalem who come to console the two sisters. Like the chorus in a classical Greek drama, they provide a wider audience, commenting on the action. In the end they illustrate the varying reactions of belief and unbelief provoked by Jesus' work. In this role they take over from the disciples, of whom we hear no more. Of the two sisters, Mary seems more associated with the Jews, particularly in the common grieving (cf. v. 33). Martha, on the other hand, enters immediately upon a distinctive journey of faith.

4. Jesus and Martha: vv. 20-27.

At this point we approach the center of the drama, with Jesus' word of revelation in vv. 25-26 constituting the theological—though not the dramatic—climax of the whole. In her encounter with Jesus Martha becomes the chief vehicle of the evangelist's theology.

a) V.20: The meeting: *When Martha heard that Jesus was coming, she went and met him, while Mary sat in the house.*

This statement introduces a contrast between the two sisters that appears to be central to the evangelist's dramatic plan. Martha responds immediately to the presence of Jesus and goes out to meet him. Mary sits in the house, adopting the posture of grieving that will characterize her throughout the episode (vv. 31, 33).[6] The varying reactions of the two sisters corresponds to the characterization of each emerging from Luke 10:38-42—more active Martha, more passive Mary. But by separating the two sisters at this point physically as well, the evangelist ensures that his teaching about the meaning of the sign (vv. 21-27) is given apart from the raising which will symbolically enact it.

b) Vv. 21-22: [21]*Martha said to Jesus, "Lord, if you had been here, my brother would not have died.* [22]*And even now I know that whatever you ask from God, God will give you."*

On meeting Jesus, Martha in her grief voices a gentle word of remonstrance (v. 21). There is a sense of disappointment with Jesus—a disappointment made all the more poignant for the reader who knows that the delay of Jesus has been deliberate. But implicit in her disappointment is also a note of faith. If he had been here, he could have prevented Lazarus from dying. Her faith is at least such as to believe that the presence of Jesus has the power to rescue from grave illness (cf. the faith of the royal official: 4:46-54). But, unlike her sister Mary, who later (v. 32) states simply the same complaint, Martha shows her openness to further possibilities. She adds (v. 22) an expression of confidence that "even now" God will grant whatever Jesus asks.

How are we to assess this further level of faith on Martha's part? What is it that she dares to hope Jesus might ask from God? With Lazarus four days dead and buried surely only his raising could be in view. Yet her responses later in the dialogue (v. 24, v. 27) and above all her eventual reluctance to open the tomb (v. 39) seem to argue strongly that she does not envisage such a remedy at all.

Determining the precise nature of Martha's faith is a critical problem throughout this section. The evangelist is either being inconsistent or—more likely—deliberately elusive and vague. He has Martha express the common human reaction to bereavement that all, and particularly believers, share—a keen sense of powerlessness and the absence of God ("Lord, if you had been here, . . . "). At the same time he has Martha express, not a specific hope (that her brother be raised), but an open-ended, generalized confidence that God can and will do something more. In this Martha can model far more effectively a journey of faith upon which all believers faced with death must go: they do not ask for the physical raising of their loved ones, but they are nonetheless to hope that in a context of faith in God this is not simply the end. Martha's hope is formulated more as a confession than a request.[7]

c) Vv. 23-24: [23]*Jesus said to her, "Your brother will rise again."* [24]*Martha said to him, "I know that he will rise again in the resurrection at the last day."*

Jesus' initial response to Martha's implicit request is again ambiguous. This paves the way for a misunderstanding on her part that will both elicit and be the foil for the climactic word of revelation. Jesus assures Martha that her brother will rise again. She takes this as a word of comfort stemming from popular religious belief in the general resurrection at the last day. He is simply offering her the consolation of conventional religion. In terms of the drama that is unfolding, however, Jesus' words foretell what is about to happen not on the last day but brought forward to this present time and place. The reader can sense this meaning and so feel the irony of Jesus' response.

At the same time, by making Jesus appear to give consolation in terms of the conventional Jewish eschatology and by having Martha give even more explicit utterance (v. 24) to that same hope, the evangelist sharpens a contrast very central to his purpose. This is the contrast between the standard future eschatology shared by Jews and Christians alike and the present or realized eschatology about to be proclaimed in the word of revelation to follow. It is in a context of that conventional belief and the somewhat lame consolation that it offers that Jesus dramatically announces the presence here and now of resurrection and life.

d) Vv. 25-26ab: The word of revelation:

[25]*Jesus said to her:*
  I am the resurrection and the life:

[*A*] *He who believes in me, even if he dies, he will live.*
[*B*] [26] *And whoever lives and believes in me will never die.*

Jesus' word of revelation comes in the form of an "I am" statement followed by a couplet which enlarges upon its implications for believers. The "I am" statement is of the predicative form familiar from other Johannine contexts where a climactic point of revelation has been reached: "I am the Bread of Life" (6:35, 51); "I am the Light of the world" (8:12; cf. 9:5); "I am the Gate" (10:7, 9); "I am the Good Shepherd" (10:11, 14); "I am the Vine" (15:1, 5). These statements proclaim not so much what Jesus is in himself, as what he is or can be for believers. The predicate ("Resurrection," "Life," "Bread," etc.) refers above all to what he has to give or communicate to the world. In a context where resurrection in terms of the conventional hope has been spoken of, Jesus suddenly claims to be personally the communicator of resurrection life and—as the couplet makes clear—to be able to communicate that benefit here and now.

In this revelation of himself as "the resurrection and the life" Jesus completely outstrips the horizons of his conversation with Martha hitherto. Up to this point only the death of Lazarus and his eventual rising at the last day had been in view. What Jesus announces here is something of universal significance—a gift for the human race of which the raising of Lazarus when it comes will be only a sign and symbol. What Jesus will be for Lazarus he can be for all who die. What he can be for the grieving Martha, he can be for all who grieve. The simple miracle story is at this point becoming a revelatory discourse with significance for all.

The couplet that follows unfolds this wider meaning. The first line (v. 25c), "He who believes in me, even if he dies, he will live," announces that if a person believes in Jesus that person's physical death cannot annul life as death normally does. There is a gift of eternal life that transcends death and carries on. Perhaps we should translate, " ... even if he dies, he will still be alive."[8] Jesus and Martha and indeed the whole company in this scene are confronting the fact of death, the death of one person, Lazarus. Outwardly, the immediate remedy would seem to be to restore Lazarus to life here and now—and this Jesus will shortly do. But Jesus is inviting

Martha to move beyond this immediate problem and contemplate a deeper truth. If Lazarus is restored simply to this
life, he will live for a time and then die again; it will be a
marvel but not a lasting remedy. Jesus uses this present pre-
dicament to draw Martha, and all who share both her faith
and her grief, to a vision where death is seen to be conquered,
not by a return to present mortal life, but by the gift of "eternal
life"—which perdures even in the face of death. Lazarus'
death—and shortly his raising—will be a symbol of this vastly
wider truth.[9]

The second line of the couplet (v. 26) basically repeats the
same statement about the believer—but this time the starting
point is not death but life. We can translate it somewhat more
freely so as to read, "And everyone who lives believing in me
shall not die for ever." The reference here is to ordinary human
life.[10] Those who are alive and whose lives are essentially
determined by faith in Jesus do not face the prospect of death
in any ultimate sense. Though their physical mortality remains,
though they will in fact actually die, already their faith ensures
that they are living the life of eternity: in this sense they "shall
not die for ever."

So, pausing to look over the couplet as a whole, we can
recognize that the concepts of death and life are both being
used in two senses: in an ordinary, physical sense and in a
spiritual, eternal sense. The two senses do not run simply in
parallel, but one (the ordinary) functions as a symbol of the
other. The pronouncement Jesus makes about death, life and
faith prepares us to understand the impending restoration of
ordinary physical life to Lazarus as a symbol of the eternal life
which Jesus, as "the resurrection and the life," communicates
now to believers.

The claim Jesus makes here finds a helpful commentary in
what he says towards the end of the discourse following the
third sign, the healing of the paralytic at the pool in chap. 5:

[24]Truly, truly, I say to you,
he who hears my word and believes him who sent me,
has eternal life;
he does not come into judgment, but has passed from
death to life.

In this earlier sign Jesus had claimed to be "ever at work" as his Father is "at work," sustaining creation (v. 17). He is not merely the agent of eschatological judgment in the sense of conventional messianic hope. He is here and now the communicator of eschatological life to believers. Those who believe in him have broken through the eschatological barrier. For them he is here and now "the resurrection and the life." They "have" eternal life already within their grasp.

In this way the more explicit statement of "realized" eschatology in 5:24 brings out the "realized" aspect implicit in the "I am" statement of 11:25. The true solution to the problem of death, exemplified in Lazarus, is at hand through faith in Jesus. He does not take away physical death; he lets believers die, as he let Lazarus die. But he communicates to believers before they die an "eternal life" transcending death. This is the high point of the revelation.

e) Vv. 26c-27: Martha's final act of faith.
26c Do you believe this? 27 She said to him, "Yes, Lord, I believe that you are the Christ, the Son of God, he who is coming into the world."

Following his self-revelation as "the resurrection and the life" Jesus questions Martha as to whether she believes this. Let us note, she is not asked whether she believes in him (and usually in the Fourth Gospel Jesus himself is the object of faith). She is asked precisely whether she believes in "this," that is, in what he has been saying. Martha says, "Yes," but goes on to fill out her response with what amounts to a confession of Jesus' status in terms of three stock titles: "Christ" (Messiah); "Son of God"; "the One who is coming into the world."

What at this point is the level of Martha's faith? The first two titles reappear in the climactic statement of purpose found at the end of the gospel: "... these are written that you may believe that Jesus is the Christ, the Son of God, and that believing you may have life in his name" (20:31). This suggests that coming to faith in Jesus in terms of these titles achieves the gospel's final aim. The titles "Messiah," "Son of God" would then bear full christological weight and Martha's use of them reveal a faith fully responsive to the exalted revelation of Jesus.[11]

Matters, however, are not so simple. Even the first two titles can be understood in a "purely messianic" sense, that is, as expressing simply conventional messianic expectation. We find this for "Son of God" early in the gospel when Nathaniel, having confessed Jesus in these terms (1:49), is told that his faith journey must proceed (1:50-51: "greater things than this you shall see"). The third title, "He who is coming into the world," corresponds to the crowd's confession of Jesus at the close of the multiplication of the loaves (6:14). This again is not an adequate expression of faith. It remains possible, then, that Martha is confessing Jesus within categories that are still simply messianic. Though proceeding in her faith journey, she has not yet grasped the full meaning of Jesus' revelation.[12]

Two things suggest that this may in fact be the case. Firstly, Martha's subsequent hesitation about opening the tomb (v. 39) is not altogether compatible with full faith in what Jesus has just revealed. Jesus, at that point, has to remind her to keep on believing in order to see the glory of God. Secondly, and here the evidence is more circumstantial, it would follow a certain pattern established in other signs/discourses if the main character persists in misunderstanding for a time. So, despite his self-revelation, the Samaritan woman goes off still wondering whether Jesus might be the Messiah (4:29). So, more seriously, the crowd in the "Bread of Life" discourse never really accepts his teaching; in the end (6: 66-67) only the Twelve remain and one could ask whether even Peter's confession ("You are the Holy One of God": 6:69) is fully adequate. By leaving misunderstanding hanging in the air the evangelist sustains suspense and sharpens awareness of the heights to which faith must go. If Martha's faith is perfect at this point, the actual sign (the raising) becomes, at least for her, superfluous. If she has still some way to go in her journey of faith, then the sign is not an anticlimax but something which reveals the glory of God. It will bring out the full meaning of what has been stated in an anticipatory way in the word of revelation.

So the chief discourse breaks off, with no further response from Jesus. Martha has still further to go in her faith. But the action is now to be carried forward by the parallel exchange between Jesus and her sister, Mary.

5. Jesus and Mary: Vv. 28-32.

a) Vv. 28-30: The summons and response of Mary:
28 When she had said this, she went and called her sister, Mary, saying quietly, "The Teacher is here and is calling for you." 29 And when she heard it, she rose quickly and went to him.

Martha sets up the scene for her sister Mary's encounter with Jesus by returning to the house and summoning her. The news she conveys about the presence of Jesus ("The Teacher is here . . .") has a particular poignancy in view of her earlier complaint (v. 21), to be repeated by Mary (v. 32), that Jesus *had* not been there when, in their understanding, his presence could saved their brother. He is present now and calling Mary. But why did he not come when they called him? We are reminded again of the keen sense of divine absence at the crucial moment and of the way in which the Johannine Jesus moves only at his own initiative, following the fixed program of his mission.

Up till this, Mary had remained within the house, locked in grief (v 20b) and surrounded, presumably, by the Jews who had come to offer consolation. It is presumably their presence that accounts for the fact that Martha speaks her message "quietly." Mary, it seems, has to escape from their concern if she is to share her sister's experience of speaking privately with Jesus. The swiftness of her response is stressed (v. 29, v. 31). Hearing the summons she rises and takes her grief to Jesus.

V. 30: *Now Jesus had not yet come to the village, but was still in the place where Martha had met him.*

This sentence simply clarifies the precise location of Jesus at this stage. In literary terms the information should perhaps have been given much earlier. But the evangelist may want us to understand that Jesus has stopped short of entering the house because he is aware that it is full of consolers and he wants to speak to the sisters in private.

b) V. 31: The misunderstanding and following of the Jews:

When the Jews who were with her in the house, consoling her,
saw Mary rise quickly and go out, they followed her, supposing
that she was going to the tomb to weep there.

It is not that "the Jews" are notably hostile at this point. But
one gains the impression that they dog Mary's tracks and seek
to contain her in her grief. This, presumably, is why they
follow immediately when she leaves (v. 31)—because they think
she is going to the tomb to weep. Mary, in her struggle for
faith, in some sense has to shake them off, emancipate herself
from the customary grieving—and nothing more than
grieving—with which the Jews as consolers surround her. In
effect, their following of her to where Jesus is ensures that the
full "cast" is "on stage" for the final act.

c) V. 32: Mary's obeisance and remonstrance before Jesus:
Then Mary, when she came where Jesus was and saw him, fell
at his feet, saying to him, "Lord, if you had been here, my
brother would not have died."

Mary's encounter with Jesus is a poor, truncated piece
compared with Martha's. It could even appear superfluous in
the extreme. But, as explained earlier, any dialogue or verbal
revelation the second encounter might have contained is re-
placed by the movement to the sign, which will enact the
earlier revelation. The two encounters stand in parallel. The
full revelation lies in the interplay between them.

Mary echoes her sister's word of remonstrance, "Lord, if
you had been here, ..." The repetition, with its implication
that the two sisters had extensively shared their disappointment, powerfully draws attention once more to the (as we
know, deliberate) absence of Jesus. Mary, like Martha, has
sufficient faith to know that his presence would have made a
difference. Her faith, however, does not proceed to an open-
ended hope as does her sister's (v. 22). Far more enveloped in
her grief, she falls at Jesus' feet. The gesture displays extremity
of emotion.

Where Martha, then, shows readiness to move on from
grief and journey further in her faith, Mary seems locked
simply in regret at Jesus' former absence and her present grief.

She does indeed leave the Jews and go to Jesus, but only the miracle can revive her faith. In contrast, Martha's growing faith will accompany the progress to the sign and see the glory (v. 40). The evangelist probably intends to instruct us through the contrast in terms of faith which the two sisters provide.

6. The Raising of Lazarus: Vv. 33-44

The encounters with both sisters concluded, the action now moves towards the dramatic climax. Before the actual raising of Lazarus, however, the evangelist pauses to dwell at some length upon the emotional reaction of those taking part—the chief focus resting upon Jesus himself.

a) Vv. 33-35: The emotional reactions of Jesus:
33 *When Jesus saw her weeping and the Jews who came with her also weeping, he was deeply moved in spirit and troubled;* 34*and he said, "Where have you laid him?" They said to him, "Lord, come and see." *35*Jesus wept.*

In the sequence making up vv. 33-38a there are no less than four clear references to Jesus' emotional reaction. In the opening sentence Jesus is "deeply moved in spirit (1) and troubled" (2). Later (v. 35) we are told that he wept (3). Finally, as Jesus comes to the tomb, he is "deeply moved again" (4). In addition to these explicit references, the remarks of the Jews (vv. 36-37) are a direct commentary upon the emotional reaction of Jesus. The evangelist seems to be underlining something very important here.

Nonetheless, while the prominence of the motif is clear, it is not so easy to decide what exactly were the emotions experienced by Jesus at this point and, secondly, find their cause. Let us take up these questions in turn.

That Jesus' response contained an element of grief is clear from the subsequent statement that he wept (v. 35). With the remaining three expressions of emotion the situation is more complex. The translation (RSV) given above for the first, "deeply moved in spirit," rather smooths over the force of the original. The Greek verb used here, *embrimasthai*, means to make a sound in an outward show of anger - to snort or the like. Here the evangelist restricts the sense to an interior movement by adding the phrase "in spirit." A similar addition —"in himself"—achieves the same effect in v. 38. Nonetheless, in both places, as in usages elsewhere in the Bible (Dan 11:30; Mark 1:43 parallel Matt 9:30 [Jesus' stern charge to the leper he has cured]; Mark 14:5), the expression has a clear reference to anger.[13] The remaining expression "troubled" (literally "troubled himself") refers to a less defined, but profound emotional disturbance. It occurs again in 12:27 and 13:21, the reference being in each case to Jesus' emotional reaction at the prospect of death. Putting all this together, we can conclude that the evangelist wishes to communicate that Jesus at this point undergoes a deep emotional stirring, one which involved not only grief, but a powerful surge of anger as well.

But what occasions Jesus' anger at this point? The statement in v. 33 implies that it was the sight of Mary's grief and that of the Jews who were with her that provokes Jesus' emotional reaction. This has suggested to many interpreters that what is making Jesus angry is the lack of faith which their profound grief seems to show. They simply grieve over the dead (the Greek verb *klaiein* can express demonstrative outward wailing), with no flicker of hope such as Martha has displayed (v. 22).[14] Moreover, the final reference to Jesus' anger (v. 38) seems to follow further skeptical remarks of the Jews (vv. 36-37).

There is a good deal to be said for this explanation of Jesus' anger. But it is somewhat hard to square with the fact that Jesus himself weeps and therefore seems to share the general grief. While Jesus' reaction is clearly a response to the general grieving, it seems to be provoked by something more complex than simple lack of faith.[15]

The clue lies perhaps in the second expression "troubled" (himself). As we have noted above, this same term recurs in 12:27, where Jesus sensing (through the arrival of the Greeks, vv. 20-23) that his hour of glorification has come, cries out, "Father, save me from this hour." This is only a moment of hesitation, because immediately he goes on to add, "No, for this purpose I have come to this hour. Father, glorify thy name." Nonetheless, the cry does represent a shrinking from the prospect of death, something which corresponds to the motif of the agony in the garden found in the synoptic gospels and echoed also in Heb 5:7-8. Similarly, the third reference to Jesus' being "troubled" occurs at the Supper at the point when Jesus announces that one of the Twelve is to betray him (13:21). All this suggests that the being "troubled" of Jesus in the present passage (11:33) has something to do with the prospect of his death. How, then, are we to link it with the other emotions—anger and grief—so as to gain a coherent rationale of Jesus' feelings at this point?

We can do this, I think, if we understand the being "troubled" as arising particularly out of the sense of being torn between two conflicting emotions. Jesus genuinely feels an empathy with those who weep for Lazarus. His weeping (v. 35) as he takes up the invitation to come and see the tomb manifests genuine sorrow (though by using a different Greek word [*dakruein*, as opposed to *klaiein*] for Jesus' reaction, the evangelist carefully distinguishes his response from the more strident grief of Mary and the Jews). Jesus, then, weeps at their grief, but their very grief intensifies the pressure upon him to restore Lazarus to them. At the same time as he feels this pressure he also knows that performing such a miracle will inevitably set in motion forces leading to death for himself. He is torn, then, between love for his friend and sympathy for the bereaved, on the one hand, and the shrinking from death that is part of human nature, on the other. His anger arises out of the impossible situation he is in and out of the conflict with the power of darkness now before him.

What the evangelist achieves by depicting the complex of Jesus' emotions is to underline the *cost* to Jesus of the action he is about to perform. This is only to continue a theme that has been prominent in the episode from the start: that Jesus is placing his own life in mortal danger by journeying to Judea to come to Lazarus and the sisters. Now we are powerfully shown how personally and how bitterly the cost sheets home to Jesus. The triumph of love over natural desire for self-preservation is not a facile, play-acting sort of thing. Jesus gives life to the one he loves by taking steps which he clearly foresees will cost his own life. This is the essential message of the elaborate description of his emotions as he makes his way to Lazarus' grave.[16]

b) Vv. 36-37: Reaction of the Jews.
[36]*So the Jews said, "See how he loved him!"* [37]*But some of them said, "Could not he who opened the eyes of the blind man have kept this man from dying?"*

The divided reactions of the Jews (vv. 36-37) precisely underline this point of conflict in Jesus. On the one hand, they (correctly) perceive his tears to be a sign of his love for Lazarus. On the other hand, others of them, in a way reminiscent of the sisters' opening complaints (v. 21, v. 32), point out the seeming incompatibility between his love and his failure to take action when action might have had some success: could not he who opened the eyes of the blind man have kept this man from dying? In view of what Jesus is about to do, this remark is highly ironical; it also considerably heightens the drama. Yes, Jesus did fail to keep this man from dying, failed to work the (lesser) miracle of healing, which all knew he could effect. But this was only to leave the way open for a stupendous miracle which they cannot even suspect. Love has indeed let the loved one die - but only to work, in the midst of grief, a far greater wonder.

c) V. 38: The journey to the tomb:

Then Jesus, deeply moved again, came to the tomb; it was a cave, and a stone lay upon it.

As Jesus approaches the tomb the evangelist again reminds us that he does so in a state of profound emotional disturbance. We have discussed the nature of this emotion above. Before it was the sight of the others mourning and the prospect of going to the tomb that appeared to trigger Jesus' emotion. Whether the new surge of emotion is caused by the skeptical comments of the Jews (vv. 36-37) or the arrival at the tomb is not clear. In any case we are made aware that the same emotion continues right up to the tomb itself.

The evangelist spends some time describing the nature of the tomb. He wants the reader to be able to picture clearly the drama that is about to unfold. The use of caves, both natural and artificial, was common in Jewish burial practice. A horizontal or vertical shaft was cut to give access to the cave and then sealed after burial with a large boulder. Which type of shaft, horizontal or vertical, led to Lazarus' tomb is not clear. However, the drama to follow, with Lazarus coming forth of his own accord, is more easily imagined on the supposition of a horizontal access to the tomb. More important, perhaps, in the evangelist's mind are parallels with the tomb of Jesus. The Johannine Easter tradition seems to presuppose that Jesus was buried in a cave with a horizontal opening (cf. 20:1-12). The large stone that sealed the entrance is mentioned also in the synoptic tradition (Matt 27:60,66; 28:2; Mark 15:46; 16:3-4; Luke 24:2), but the Fourth Evangelist employs a different word to describe its removal (Greek verb *hairein*)—the same word used with reference to the opening of the tomb of Lazarus (11:39, 41).

d) Vv. 39-41a: Before the Tomb: the hesitation and the opening.

[39]*Jesus said, "Take away the stone." Martha, the sister of the dead man, said to him, "Lord by this time there will be an odor, for he has been dead four days."[40] Jesus said to her, "Did I not tell you that if you would believe you would see the glory of God?"[41a] So they took away the stone.*

We now stand before the dramatic climax of the whole. The evangelist has already built up the intensity by dwelling at such length upon the emotions of all present, including Jesus. Now, above all in a Jewish context which, apart from the general horror of corruption, held burial places to be ritually unclean, we face the awful prospect of opening a tomb.

Whatever his feelings hitherto, Jesus' command is now firm and direct, indicating a decision clearly made. Confronting the realm of death, he shows the total self-possession and authority which in this gospel are a feature especially of the passion. Here the stone is to be taken away at his command. At *his* tomb Mary Magdalene will find the stone already mysteriously removed (20:1).

Martha's understandable hesitation to remove the stone (v. 39b) heightens the drama still further. Her explanation reinforces the sense of horror at the prospect of opening the tomb. Not only will there be an odor,[17] but, as we have already seen, it was commonly held that by the fourth day after death corruption would have set in to such an extent as to render the features of the deceased unrecognizable. It was not her brother that Martha was going to see. For this, according to conventional belief (v. 24), she had to await the general resurrection. Her hesitation at this point strongly suggests that she has not grasped the full meaning of Jesus' earlier word of revelation (vv. 25-26), that here and now Jesus is "the resurrection and the life," who will display this truth symbolically by raising her brother from the dead.

Jesus' response to Martha (v. 40) is at first sight odd. Nowhere has he promised her precisely that if she believed she would see the glory of God. His words in fact recall his initial statement to the disciples that Lazarus' illness was for the glory of God (v. 4) and also his subsequent remark that it would provide for them an opportunity of faith (v. 15). The response is, however, intended to uncover the true depth of the act he is about to perform. All the bystanders, those who believe and those who do not, will witness the raising of Lazarus. They will in this sense see the miracle. But only those whose seeing is accompanied by deep faith will penetrate beneath the miracle to grasp the true Johannine "sign." Martha and all those prepared to join her journey of faith will see more than a marvellous anticipation of the general resurrection. They will discern a revelation of the power and presence ("glory") of God as they come to see in Jesus here and now "the resurrection and the life."

"They" take away the stone (v. 41a). In having the stone removed ("they" presumably includes servants or bystanders) the sisters already give expression to the faith required by Jesus. Like the servants at the wedding in Cana, who draw water from the jars at Jesus' command and take it to the master of the feast (2:8), like the royal steward who goes home simply believing Jesus' word that his son would live (4:50), those who remove the stone act out a faith responsive simply to the word of Jesus. In their preparedness to confront the full horror of death their faith accompanies, it does not rest upon, the sign. Such a faith finds even in death a vision of God's glory.

f) Vv. 41b-42: The Prayer of Jesus:

[41b] *And Jesus lifted up his eyes and said, "Father, I thank thee that thou has heard me. [42] I knew that thou hearest me always, but I have said this on account of the people standing by, that they may believe that thou didst send me."*

Nowhere else in the gospel tradition does Jesus pray to the Father before working a miracle. What we have here, however, is not strictly a prayer, but a thanksgiving, an act of communion with the Father which the bystanders are allowed to "overhear." Jesus thanks the Father for having heard him and hearing him always. Through this prayer the evangelist reminds us that Jesus' whole ministry has been nothing but a working out of the life-giving mission he has from the Father (4:34; 6:38; 10:10b,18; 14:31; 15:10; 17:2; 19:30) and a continuation on earth of the eternal communion between them (1:1,18).[18]

Both the gesture preceding this prayer, lifting up the eyes, and the initial invocation have a striking parallel in the opening words of Jesus' extended prayer in chap. 17:

"When Jesus had spoken these words, he lifted up his eyes to heaven and said, 'Father, the hour has come; glorify thy Son that the Son may glorify thee, since thou has given him power over all flesh, to give eternal life to all whom thou hast given him'" (vv. 1-2).

What Jesus is now about to do, which of course hastens the path to his own death, anticipates the mutual glorification of Father and Son achieved upon the cross. Bringing Lazarus back to earthly life is a symbol of the supreme glorification, from which life will flow to all believers. Jesus prays, then, not for power to work the miracle, but for the faith of the bystanders—that they will see beyond the miracle something of this fuller meaning bound up with the mysterious communion of Father and Son. Ultimately it is the status of Jesus, as the one who has from the Father the power to give life (5:21, 26; 17:2), that is in view.

Vv. 43-44: The Raising of Lazarus:

43 When he had said this, he cried with a loud voice, "Lazarus, come out." 44 The dead man came out, his hands and feet bound with bandages, and his face wrapped with a cloth. Jesus said to them, "Unbind him, and let him go."

Jesus' essential union with the Father established through this prayer, the way is now clear for a rather matter-of-fact description of the raising. But the very simplicity of the language actually heightens the drama. Jesus cries out "with a loud voice." The strength of the cry connotes authority. But by it we are probably also to understand that Jesus is, as he earlier purposed (v. 11), awakening Lazarus from sleep—the sleep of death. At a deeper level, however, his voice, resounding throughout the realm of death, issues a general summons to eternal life. The calling forth of Lazarus enacts an earlier prophecy—the hour "when the dead hear the voice of the Son of God and live" (5:25), "when all who are in the tombs hear his voice and come forth" (5:28). Lazarus heeds Jesus' cry as an anticipation of all who will rise at the general resurrection. In a more "realized" sense his coming back to life symbolizes the power of Jesus to be for all believers here and now "the resurrection and the life."

The evangelist dwells at some length upon the appearance of Lazarus emerging from the grave (v. 44). Though in some fashion able to move, the wrappings of death still envelop him. Totally passive, his hands and feet bound in bandages, his face wrapped with a napkin (*soudarion*), he cannot be fully restored to human life until he is unbound and let go free.

There is one other place in the gospel where the wrappings of death feature strongly. This is the scene where Peter and the Beloved Disciple come to the empty tomb of Jesus (20:3-10). Looking into the tomb from the outside the Beloved Disciple saw the linen cloths (*othonia*) lying there (v. 5). But when he went into the tomb he saw something more, already seen by Peter (vv. 6-7): the napkin (*soudarion*) which had been on Jesus' head, not lying with the cloths, but rolled up in a place by itself. Straightaway, we are told (v. 9), "he saw and he believed." What he saw constituted for him a sign of resurrection. The neatly folded, separately placed napkin convinced him that here was no evidence of grave robbery but instead of an active, free, majestic resumption of life. Jesus, who had laid down his life of his own accord, had exercised a similar power to take it up again (10:18).[19]

Considering together the two "raising" contexts (John 11 and John 20) where in each case so much is made of the apparel of the grave, it is hard to escape the conclusion that the evangelist wants us to see a contrast. The napkin (*soudarion*) is the link. Lazarus is raised totally passive, summoned by the command of Jesus, needing to be loosed from the bonds of death, which include the *soudarion* covering his face. This contrasts sharply with the active rising of Jesus, who removes from his face, neatly folds and sets aside the cloth that had covered him in death. In this way the raising of Lazarus functions as an anticipatory foil for the presentation of Jesus' own resurrection. Lazarus receives a summons back to life from Jesus. Jesus, who gave his life that he might raise Lazarus, takes back the life he has from the Father.

The whole drama ends, then, with these two commands of Jesus: the summons to Lazarus to come forth from the grave and the command to the community to remove from him the bonds of death. Jesus has restored Lazarus to earthly life. But on the deeper level that we have attempted to keep in mind all along, he has provided a symbol of his claim to be for all believers "the resurrection and the life." The community, who now take an active role in the miracle by stripping away the bonds of death, should come to recognize the deeper meaning of the "sign."

7. Vv. 45-46: The Reaction of the Jews

⁴⁵*Many of the Jews therefore, who had come with Mary and had seen what he did, believed in him;*⁴⁶ *but some of them went to the Pharisees and told them what Jesus had done.*

Most miracle stories end by giving an indication of the reaction on the part of the bystanders or crowd. This one is no exception. But in a way that is typically Johannine and in fact parallels an earlier reaction to Jesus' grief (v. 37), the bystanders' response goes in two directions. Positively (v. 45), "many of the Jews ... who had come with Mary" believe in Jesus on the basis of what they had seen. That is, they show the kind of faith that follows signs - a faith regarded as inadequate elsewhere in the gospel (2:23-25; 4:48; 6:26). Such an attitude is at least a beginning. Mary, interestingly enough, is still being associated with these Jews who had come to console her. This suggests that from the outset her journey from simple grief to faith has hardly outstripped theirs; she believes on the basis of the sign. In her believing and that of these bystanders, the purpose of the miracle as stated by Jesus to the disciples earlier on (v. 15) has been fulfilled.

Alongside this positive reaction, however, stands a negative and, in the end, fatal response. Some of the Jews go off and tell the Pharisees what Jesus has done. In this they are perhaps more naive than malevolent. Presumably they do not deny the fact of the miracle—that Lazarus has been brought to life. But for them it is simply a fact, the political consequences of which are more significant than any deeper meaning.

The Aftermath: 11:47—12:19.

1. The Plot against Jesus (11:47-53).

The plot that follows the raising of Lazarus (vv. 47-53) not only sets in motion the events leading to Jesus' death but also brings out the fuller meaning of that death. The authorities fear that through his signs Jesus will win an ever wider allegiance. Then the whole people will come under threat from Rome (v. 48). In the context of this apprehension for the safety of the whole nation the High Priest, Caiaphas, makes his pragmatic observation: it is better that one man should die for the people, so that the whole nation might not perish (v. 50). Straightaway the evangelist points out the irony encased in this advice. Here is the chief religious figure of the nation promoting Jesus' death and, despite himself, spelling out in the same words the true meaning of that death. Jesus is not to die simply as an individual messianic pretender nor because he gave life to an individual - Lazarus. He is to die in order to give life to a whole people and, in a wider vision still, so that all the "children of God" might be gathered into one (v. 52).

The in-gathering of the scattered "children of God" recalls the motif of the eschatological gathering of the scattered children (Diaspora) of Israel. But the evangelist undoubtedly includes here a reference to believers from the Gentile world as well. As Jesus later prophesies (12:32), when he is "lifted up" (in death), he will draw all people to himself. For this reason the sign upon his cross must be written not only in Hebrew but also in the languages—Latin and Greek—which will make it readable to the whole world (19:20). So Lazarus, whom Jesus calls to life at the cost of his own life upon the cross, becomes a type, a representative of a world-wide company of believers.

2. The Anointing at Bethany (12:1-8).

It is to underline this "typical" role of Lazarus that the evangelist has his story continue somewhat beyond the actual raising. The anointing of Jesus' feet (12:1-8) takes place in Bethany six days before the fateful Passover. Twice (v. 1, v. 2) we are told that Lazarus is present. Indeed, it is his sisters who host the meal. True to the pattern emerging also from Luke 10:38-42, Martha takes the active part—serving at table— while Mary performs a service of loving devotion to Jesus: she anoints his feet with costly ointment and wipes them with her hair (v. 3).

In the context of Jesus' own movement towards his death, Mary's loving service is totally appropriate. Jesus has given life to her brother—but has done so at the cost of his own life, a cost soon to be required. By anointing his feet with costly ointment (so costly that its aroma fills the whole room), Mary shows both that she appreciates the cost and that she is ready to offer something costly in return. Lazarus, the first beneficiary of Jesus' death, is present to see it all. But, again, he stands in for, he represents all who down the ages will receive the gift of life from Jesus.

3. The Plot against Lazarus (12:9-11).

Lazarus, however, has still more of his somewhat passive

role to play. In the short passage (12:9-11) that forms a bridge to the account of the triumphant entry, we are told that great crowds of the Jews came out to Bethany, not only on account of Jesus but also to see Lazarus, whom he had raised from the dead (v. 9). In this they exhibit the kind of curiosity in the marvellous, rather than response to the person of Jesus, which the evangelist tends to downgrade. More seriously, their interest in Lazarus moves the authorities to resolve to put him to death as well, since his restoration is leading "many of the Jews" to go away and believe in Jesus (v. 11). In this we find another respect in which Lazarus becomes a type for all subsequent believers. As beneficiary of Jesus' gift of life, he comes under threat from the authorities. In this he foreshadows the hostility which the Johannine community will itself later experience (15:18-21; 16:2-4). Life is not given or received without cost.

4. The Triumphant Entry (12:12-19).

Finally, in the course of the actual entry (12:19), we are told that the crowd that had been with Jesus when he raised Lazarus from the dead bore witness (v. 17) and that the reason for their enthusiasm was his working of "this sign" (v. 18). All this provokes from "the Pharisees" a further cry of desperation: "You see that you can do nothing; look, the world is going after him (v. 19). The irony ("[whole] world") is again clear. So also is their motivation: they see their power, their hold upon the people fast slipping from their grasp. Here, then, for the third time the evangelist reminds us that it is the raising of Lazarus that particularly sets in motion the process leading to Jesus' death. In giving life Jesus threatens worldly power. The raising of Lazarus is not simply a conquest of death in one isolated instance. It is a potent sign, a symbol that Jesus effectively challenges all the forces of death mounted by the world.[20]

4

The Composition of John 11:1-46: Did Jesus Raise Lazarus From the Dead?

So far we have taken the story of the raising of Lazarus more or less as a given whole proceeding from the evangelist's pen. We have noted areas where "Johannine" features seem particularly marked. But we have not attempted in any set fashion to distinguish material which might be attributed to the evangelist from that which might be regarded as coming from an earlier, pre-existing tradition. It remains to ask whether the evangelist simply wrote this account in its entirety (either as a free creation of the imagination or as a record of what he or others remembered of something Jesus actually did) or whether the account presupposed a rather complex process of composition, of which the contribution of the evangelist was only the summit and crown.

Intimately bound up with this question, of course, is that of the historicity of the narrative. Did Jesus raise a man called Lazarus from the dead? And if in fact he did so, did the actual event take place according to the long drama told in John 11 with its dialogues and revelatory words or did the episode take a simpler form, like the miracle stories recorded in the synoptic gospels? In the latter case the Johannine account, though historical in germ, would represent a considerable embellishment upon the original happening.

The question concerning the historicity of the Lazarus miracle can only be approached by analyzing the account from the point of view of composition. If traces of composite authorship are clearly detectable, then one must rule out the two extreme positions mentioned above: 1. that the entire story is purely a creation of the evangelist's imagination; or 2. that it is a literal report, based upon his own or some other eye-witness' memory, that he alone has set down. If elements of redaction (the evangelist) and tradition (pre-existing sources) can be found, then the path through the question of historicity lies in the careful investigation of these sources. The first task, then, must be to see whether the account in John 11:1-46 bears traces of multiple composition.

The Composition of John 11:1-46

Read through quickly, John 11:1-46, gives the impression of a skillfully constructed dramatic narrative—and so, of course, it is. When one begins to look more closely, however, traces of not-so-well-disguised stitching and patching start to appear. Most of these center around the two sisters, Martha and Mary. As we have noted already, in dramatic and theological terms it is Martha who has the major role. At times, however, traces of Mary's prominence can be discerned. In the very first sentence, for example, Lazarus is said to be "from the village of Mary and Martha, her sister." Here the reference to Martha looks a bit like an afterthought; the village is identified through Mary. The situation is quite reversed in v. 5 where we are told that "Jesus loved Martha and her sister and Lazarus"; Mary is not even mentioned by name. In v. 19 Martha receives first mention but in v. 45 "the Jews" are described as those "who had come with Mary"; Martha is not mentioned, though it is clear from v. 39 that she also is present at the tomb.

In general, then, the passages where Martha is prominent give the impression of being somewhat intrusive. Relying perhaps on the same tradition as that underlying the episode with two sisters, Martha and Mary, in Luke 10:38-42, the evangelist seems to have played up the role of Martha in a story that originally centered upon Mary. He has made Mary simply the foil for Martha, who has now become the chief character and vehicle of his own distinctive theology (notably, the realized eschatology and christological confessions in vv. 23-27, the references to faith and glory in vv. 40, 41b-42).

But traces of the evangelist's hand are not confined to material concerned with Martha. Much of the material in Jesus' two-pronged deliberation with his disciples takes up distinctive Johannine themes and really adds little to the actual narrative (see vv. 4, 7b-10, 16). Nowhere else in fact do the disciples play any part in the story. The reference to "the Jews" in v. 8 bears the technical, hostile Johannine sense. Elsewhere in this story, as we have noted, "the Jews" are simply inhabitants of Jerusalem who come out to console the sisters. Though they appear in a more benign light than is usually the case in John, references to them are introduced somewhat roughly into the narrative. The fact, too, that they form the link with the plot that follows (vv. 47-53; cf. also their reminiscence of Jesus' healing of the man born blind, v. 37) makes one suspect that their appearance has much to do with the evangelist's sense of overall dramatic unity.[1]

Other minor inconsistencies and repetitions seem to betray a process of composition. V. 2, which again refers only to Mary, contains an identification of her as "the one who anointed the Lord with oil and wiped his feet with her hair"; the reference, curiously, is set in the past, though in fact the incident is yet to take place (12:1-8). In a rather unnecessary way v. 6a repeats the reference to Jesus' hearing the message already mentioned in v. 4. Likewise Mary's words of remonstrance on meeting Jesus (v. 32b) exactly repeat what Martha had said earlier (v. 21). Martha's hesitation about opening the tomb (vv. 39b-40) and Jesus' prayer to the Father (vv. 41b-42) come between the order to take away the stone and its execution. Both appear to be Johannine features that intrude to some extent upon the narrative.

Faced, then, with what seems to be clear evidence for separating traditional material from the evangelist's own contribution, scholars have attempted to reconstruct an earlier source which would have formed the basis for the final redaction. The chief elements to be removed, as being the work of the evangelist, consist in the deliberation with the disciples (vv. 5-16), the central dialogue with Martha (vv. 18-30), Jesus' prayer to the Father (vv. 41b-42) and scattered references to "the Jews." V. 2 is also generally considered to be an afterthought, added by the evangelist to integrate the episode into the wider framework of the passion.

By eliminating this "Johannine" material, it is possible to reconstruct a simple miracle story. Granted some disagreement on detail, many scholars would see the basic content of such a story in the following reconstruction:

> [1]Now a certain man was ill, Lazarus of Bethany, the village of Mary and her sister Martha. [3]So the sisters sent to him, saying "Lord, he whom you love is ill." [4a]When Jesus heard it he said [7a]to the disciples, [11b]"Our friend Lazarus has fallen asleep, [15b]but let us go to him."
>
> [17]Now when Jesus came, he found that Lazarus had already been in the tomb four days.
>
> [32]Then Mary, when she came where Jesus was and saw him, fell at his feet, saying to him, "Lord, if you had been here, my brother would not have died." [33]When Jesus saw her weeping, he was deeply disturbed [34]and said, "Where have you laid him?" They said to him, "Lord, come and see."
>
> [38]Then Jesus came to the tomb; it was a cave, and a stone lay upon it. [39]Jesus said, "Take away the stone." [41a]So they took away the stone. [43b]He cried out with a loud voice, "Lazarus, come out." [44]The dead man came out, his hands and feet wrapped with a cloth. Jesus said to them, "Unbind him, and let him go."[2]

We may note that in this account Martha plays a very minor role. Mary is more prominent. But the dramatic high point and focus lies entirely upon the miracle of raising itself. What we have is something akin to the raising of the widow's son in Luke 7:11-17: the miracle fulfils the expectation concerning the raising of the dead in the messianic era (cf. Luke 7:22).

The agreement amongst scholars on the basic content of such an earlier account is truly impressive. There is also a widespread tendency to recognize that a text in this form (or perhaps this form slightly embellished) came to the evangelist as part of a proposed "Signs Source," which many recent scholars hold to be the chief source underlying John 1-12.[3] There is, however, disagreement on many points of detail. Above all, it is hard to state categorically that some elements occurring here are not "Johannine": for example, the invitation, "Come and see" (cf. 1:39), the description of the grave-clothes (cf. 20:6-7). By the same token it is hard to exclude from this "traditional" account so-called "Johannine" features—for example, the two-day delay (v. 6)—which are not without parallel in the synoptic tradition (cf. Jesus' delay in going to the daughter of Jairus, while he attends to the woman with a flow of blood [Mark 5:21-43 and parallels]).

In short, it seems impossible to reconstruct from the text as we now have it a fixed and certain earlier account of the Lazarus miracle which would command general agreement. Features such as the unevenness of the text and especially the treatment of Martha do indeed suggest that the evangelist has taken up and embellished a pre-existing written source. But the sure text of that source (or sources) is now embedded beyond recovery within the final version.[4]

Synoptic Material related to John 11:1-46; 12:1-8.

Even if we cannot reconstruct in precise form the tradition used by the evangelist, we can, nonetheless, enquire further about its origins. Central in this matter are the clear links which the Lazarus story in the Fourth Gospel has with traditions found in the synoptic gospels. It is helpful at this stage to pursue these connections at least briefly.

a) A Woman Anoints Jesus Shortly Before His Death.

Bethany, the village of Martha, Mary and Lazarus according to John 11:1, appears in the synoptic tradition in connection with the anointing of Jesus before his death. In Mark 14:3-9 (parallel Matt 26:6-13) an unnamed woman anoints the head of Jesus with costly ointment in the house of "Simon the Leper." This, of course, parallels very closely the anointing of Jesus by Mary at Bethany described in John 12:1-8. In Luke this tradition appears earlier in the public life (7:36-50): a woman who is a public sinner anoints Jesus in the house of "Simon, the Pharisee." There is an interesting coherence between the Lucan and the Johannine accounts of this episode in that in both the woman anoints Jesus' feet (rather than his head, as in Mark and Matthew) and wipes them with her hair. The Johannine tradition underlines this detail when at the beginning of the account of the raising of Lazarus (11:2) it identifies Mary as the one "who anointed the Lord with ointment and wiped his feet with her hair."

Clearly, then, there was a tradition, later emerging in both the synoptic and Johannine literature, that a woman publicly anointed Jesus before his death at a meal. The location at Bethany may also have belonged to an early stage of this tradition. The Fourth Evangelist identifies the woman as Mary, the sister of Martha and Lazarus, and closely associates the act she performed with the raising of her brother from the dead.

b) Martha and Mary

The synoptic material most obviously related to the Lazarus story is the episode with Martha and Mary told by Luke in 10:38-42. Jesus, on his final journey to Jerusalem, comes to an unnamed village. A woman named Martha receives him into her house and provides hospitality. Instead of helping with the serving, her sister Mary sits at the Lord's feet, listening to his teaching. For this she earns a reproof from her sister. Jesus, however, comes to her defense, saying that she has chosen "the better part." In this episode not only do the two women bear the same names as the sisters of Lazarus in John 11-12, but there is also a correspondence in the characters and activity ascribed to each. As already noted, Martha emerges from the Lazarus story as clearly the more active, aggressive character; Mary, more passive, remains in the house grieving until called by Jesus. At the subsequent meal in which the anointing takes place, Martha serves the meal, while Mary is at the feet of Jesus, anointing them.

Despite the obvious discrepancies, there is clearly much congruence between these two traditions. There are good grounds for holding that in the composition of the Lazarus sequence in John 11:1-46 (together with John 12:1-8) a tradition about two sisters, Martha and Mary, who gave hospitality to Jesus, one taking a more active, one a more passive role, played a significant part.

c) Simon the Leper

In the anointing tradition found in all three synoptic gospels the name of the person in whose house the episode takes place is "Simon." In Luke 7:36-50 the host, Simon, is a Pharisee. In Mark 14:3-9 (parallel Matt 26:6-13) the house belongs to "Simon, the Leper." It would seem that this means a healed leper, since Simon would hardly have been present had he still been suffering from the disease. The epithet, however, is interesting because there is some evidence that in the gospel milieu being healed from leprosy was considered tantamount to being raised from the dead (cf. 2 Kings 5:7). We might ask, then, whether the figure of Lazarus appearing in John 11-12 as the brother of Martha and Mary may not have some connection with the "Simon" who appears in the anointing accounts as host and owner of the house. If the tradition about the woman who anointed Jesus' feet at Bethany in the house of Simon the Leper was combined at some stage with that which told of the hospitality accorded to Jesus by two sisters, Martha and Mary, we are not far from assembling in recognizable form the key *dramatis personae* of the episodes in John 11:1-45 and 12:1-8. We have already noted that the indications in John 11 that Lazarus was in fact the brother of the two sisters (v. 2, v. 39) come in the form of additions made somewhat clumsily to an earlier account. In all likelihood it was the evangelist himself who made the male figure the brother.

But what of the name of this male figure? Did an original Simon, who had been cured (by Jesus?) from leprosy, and who hosted the meal at which the anointing was performed become at some stage "Lazarus, the brother of Martha and Mary," the man Jesus brought back from the dead? At this point we must turn to further synoptic tradition.

d) The Rich Man and Lazarus

The only other place where the name "Lazarus" appears in

the New Testament is in the second part of the parable of the Rich Man and Lazarus in Luke 16:19-31. In fact, this is the only occurrence of a proper name in any parable of Jesus. In the first part of the parable Lazarus is a poor man, who lies covered in sores (a condition similar to leprosy!) outside a rich man's house, longing to eat something from the latter's sumptuous table, but not receiving so much as a crumb. In the afterlife reversal of fate upon which the parable revolves, the rich man, now tormented in Hades, begs Abraham to send Lazarus to his brothers to warn them of the fate that awaits them if, following his example, they do not repent. Abraham replies that such a warning would not be heeded even if its messenger was to be one risen from the dead.

This parable could hardly provide a basis upon which to build up the entire Lazarus episode occurring in John 11. But it does point to a tradition linking rising from the dead with the name Lazarus. Also, as already noted, the poor man originally has a condition rather similar to leprosy. The question arises, then, whether there may not have been in circulation a tradition about Jesus' raising of a person known as Lazarus, a tradition which emerges in the name given to the beggar in Luke 16 and which has also had its influence upon the naming of the chief character of John 11. We have no evidence that Mark or Matthew had any knowledge of such a tradition, just as they seem also to have known nothing of the Nain miracle recorded by Luke. That John and Luke had a "Lazarus raised from the dead" tradition in common is of a piece with other links these two evangelists have over against the remaining synoptic tradition.[5]

Clearly, none of these links with the synoptic tradition can serve to show a direct dependence of John's Lazarus story upon the synoptic material. But there is enough evidence of shared material to make it quite plausible that the Fourth Evangelist could have known traditions closely related to those appearing in the synoptic gospels, especially Luke, and worked them up for his own purpose—notably combining a tradition about Jesus' raising of a person named Lazarus with the Bethany traditions concerning Martha and Mary and the woman who anointed Jesus' feet. To what extent the evangelist himself might have worked up these traditions, to what extent they may already have been combined in a major source used for the composition of John 11:1-46 we cannot know.

The Origins of the Tradition about the Raising of Lazarus

Did Jesus raise Lazarus from the dead? Now that we have reviewed the synoptic traditions that appear to bear relationship to the narrative in John 11:1-46, we are better placed to pursue this question.

First of all, as already noted, the unmistakable evidence that the evangelist has made use of pre-existing traditions in composing his account enables us to rule out the two extreme positions in either direction: a) that Jesus raised Lazarus from his tomb exactly as described in John 11; b) that the whole is entirely the creation of the evangelist.

These two positions excluded, the question then really centers upon the historical reliability of the tradition underlying the evangelist's account. Various solutions to this question can be imagined. 1. The tradition does take us back to a raising miracle performed by the historical Jesus so that, for all the Johannine embellishment now appearing in the account, the basic event, the raising, has a foundation in history. 2. The tradition does not go back to Jesus, but was created in the post-Easter community. 3. (A mediating position) a healing miracle of the historical Jesus has been transformed in the post-Easter tradition into a miracle of raising from the dead.[6]

There are some who would exclude the first possibility simply on the grounds that miracles, above all miracles of resurrection from the dead, do not occur. Adopting a philosophical position like this simply forecloses the question from the start. Originally proposed on the grounds of what is "scientifically" acceptable to the rational inquirer, such prejudgment about what is and is not possible in the natural order is itself increasingly coming to be rejected as "unscientific."

If, then, we keep an open mind on this matter in philosophical terms, we should be ready to accept the tradition, quite central to the gospel proclamation, that Jesus worked what in his day at least were regarded as miracles. Not only was this proclaimed by his followers. It was recognized by his adversaries and, interpreted as sorcery, used as polemic against him. There is little reason to doubt the historical reliability of the tradition about Jesus as healer and exorcist.[7]

With raising of the dead, however, we enter a separate category. We have noted two other miracles of this type attributed to Jesus in the synoptic tradition: the raising of the daughter of Jairus, told in all three gospels, and the raising of the son of the widow of Nain, told by Luke alone. There is also the inclusion of "raising the dead" in the description of Jesus' activity in his response to the disciples of John the Baptist:

> "Go and tell John what you hear and see: the blind receive their sight and the lame walk, lepers are cleansed and the deaf hear, and the dead are raised up, and the poor have the good news preached to them (Matt 11:4-5; parallel Luke 7:22).

It is generally agreed that this response, at least in germ, is an authentic word of Jesus. However, the phrase about raising the dead (as also the reference to cleansing lepers) is wanting in the Old Testament texts (Isa 29:18; 35:5; 61:1) which seem to form the basis for the response. This has led to the view that the references to raising the dead are not original but represent additions from the early church.

Of the actual raisings described in the synoptic gospels, the Nain miracle is set by Luke immediately before the response to John the Baptist (7:11-17). It seems well-placed to justify the inclusion of raising the dead among the things that the disciples "have seen and heard." The location in Nain, a Galilean village with no claim otherwise to historical or biblical significance, is perhaps the strongest factor in favor of historicity. But we have already noted the unmistakable similarity between this episode and the raising of a widow's son attributed to Elijah in 1 Kings 17:17-24. This suggests that what has been chiefly operative in the formation of Luke's story is not a genuine historical reminiscence but rather an impulse to present Jesus' works as the messianic re-enactment of the ministry of Elijah.[8]

The raising of the daughter of Jairus (Mark 5:22-24, 35-43; parallel Matt 9:18-19, 23-26; Luke 8:40-42; 49-56) has several

features suggesting a very early anchorage in the tradition—
most notably traces of an Aramaic substratum beneath the
present Greek text (cf. especially the preservation of the
Aramaic form of Jesus' command to the child [Mark 5:41]).
But again one cannot exclude the possibility that an original
account of the restoration to health of a child at the point of
death has, at a very early stage of the tradition, been transformed into an account of a raising.[9]

In short, neither the summary statement of Jesus' activity
given in the response to the Baptist, nor the two traditions
presented as actual raisings provide watertight evidence from
the synoptic tradition that Jesus actually raised the dead. In
each case we have to reckon with a tendency towards enhancement of the status and activity of Jesus as the early
church increasingly retrojected back into its memory of his
historical life a messianic aura and pattern of association that
was not, at least in explicit terms, originally there.[10] Included
within that pattern of association was belief in the general
resurrection of the dead, of which the raisings attributed to
Jesus would be seen to be both anticipation and pledge.

When we turn from this synoptic material to the Lazarus
story of the Fourth Gospel we encounter a raising tradition
enhanced further still. The raising of a person already four
days in the tomb goes considerably beyond the situation presupposed in the case of Jairus' daughter or the widow's son,
neither of whom had yet been buried. It represents a notable
broadening of the category in the claims it makes for Jesus'
power. Even if we exclude the "fourth day" detail as a Johannine embellishment, the story in its pre-Johannine form must
have centered around the tomb and so involved the bringing
back to life of a person dead and buried for some time. We
have to reckon, then, with a stupendous miracle, of which the
synoptic tradition is apparently quite unaware.

This silence of the synoptic tradition in the matter of the
raising of Lazarus has always been the chief stumbling block
for claims of historicity. If Jesus performed so stupendous an
act in the highly public way described in John 11, it is surprising that the synoptic gospels appear to know nothing of it.
Even if a simpler version of the miracle—one shorn of Johannine features such as the four-day entombment, the highly

public context, the linkage with Jesus' arrest and execution—
is ascribed to the tradition, one is left with a most notable
enhancement of any miracle known from other sources.

Various responses have been made to this problem: most
notably, that the synoptic tradition is chiefly interested in the
Galilean activity of Jesus and so might well omit or lack a
miracle located in Judea or that Jesus' power to raise the dead
had been sufficiently demonstrated in the Capernaum (Jairus)
and Nain raisings. But neither of these explanations really
meets the difficulty. If Jesus did bring Lazarus alive out of his
tomb, the silence of all sources save the Johannine is puzzling
to say the least.

In short, then, while we cannot exclude the possibility that
traditions about Jesus' raising the dead do have a basis in his
historical life, we cannot at the same time exclude the possibility, indeed the likelihood, that all such traditions, the
Lazarus story included, stem from the post-Easter church.
This is not to say that they are pure creations of the tradition
without any anchorage to history whatsoever. What is more
likely to have been the case is that stories which originally told
of healings performed by Jesus upon persons near to death or
suffering death-like diseases (such as leprosy) became, under
the force of a tendency to inflate the tradition theologically,
accounts of raisings from the dead. Along these lines the
Lazarus story, together with that of Jairus, would fall into the
third (compromise) explanation of those listed above: an
account that originally (and authentically) told of a healing
has become the story of a raising from the dead. It is now time
to relate this discussion of historicity more closely to the possible process of composition outlined above.

Many scholars hold that the origins of the Lazarus story
can be traced in the synoptic material, most notably in the
parable of the Rich Man and Lazarus in Luke 16:19-31.[11] As
we have already noted, the only other appearance of the name
Lazarus in the New Testament occurs here; also, in the final
part of the parable (vv. 27-31) the Rich Man proposes that
Lazarus return from the dead in order to convey a warning to
his brothers. The claim is made that in John 11:1-46, either
through the working of the evangelist or the tradition before
him, the Lazarus who in the parable could not return from the

dead has become historicized as a Lazarus who does return from the dead. This story has been melded with the Martha and Mary traditions also found in Luke so as to provide the complete story found in John 11, where Lazarus is the brother of the two sisters.

Whether the appendix (vv. 27-31) formed part of the original parable in Luke 16 or represents a Lucan addition is not certain. Undoubtedly it contains Lucan features, but it can also be integrated neatly into the overall structure of the parable.[12] The inclusion, however, of proper names in a parable is unprecedented. It is very likely that it is Luke who has made the poor man Lazarus and who has done so on the basis of a pre-existing tradition about a Lazarus who returned from the dead. If this is so, then it would seem that a pre-Lucan Lazarus tradition has been the source both of Luke's addition to the parable and of the Lazarus story in John 11. In this case, John 11:1-46 would not be directly dependent upon Luke 16:27-31, but both would draw upon a common tradition about a Lazarus who returned from the dead.

In the end, then, we seem to come back to an early tradition about a Lazarus brought back from the dead. It is well understandable that at a later stage, possibly at the hand of the Fourth Evangelist himself, this Lazarus tradition was combined with early forms of the Martha-Mary tradition and also with the tradition about the woman who anointed Jesus at a banquet. All three traditions combined in this way to provide a basis for the present narrative found in John 11-12. (See figure 1.)

The existence of this early "Lazarus back from the dead" tradition, now reflected in John 11 and Luke 16, is really the last step we can take with any security in the quest for a historical foundation. What the origins of this tradition were remains a matter for speculation. We cannot exclude the possibility that it does go back to a miracle of raising performed by Jesus. Something must have given rise to the existence of such a tradition and the attachment of the name Lazarus to it. But also we must reckon with the tendencies towards the enhancement of miracles reviewed at some length above.

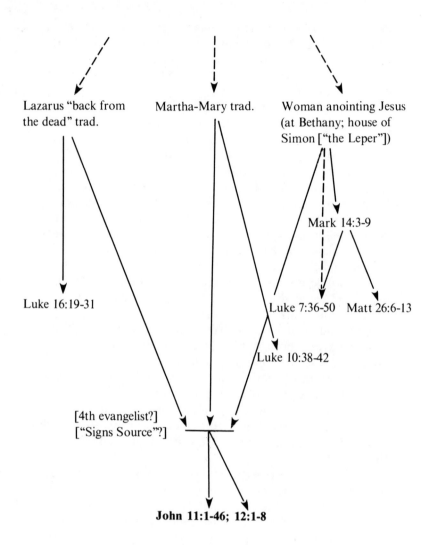

Figure 1

Finally, we must bear in mind that even if we were to believe that at the origins of the tradition stood an act of Jesus which from the start was regarded as a raising from the dead, we have not then arrived at an actual raising. For the report gives us access not to such an event in itself but to the impression the event made upon witnesses and the judgment concerning it which they formed. Such a judgment is inevitably bound up with the understanding of life and death prevailing at the time, an understanding where the barrier between life and death was not necessarily where we would draw it today. This is a question which arises in connection with all the biblical raisings.[13]

For an apologetic which looks to the miracles of Jesus to demonstrate his status as divine Son of God to lose the authenticity of the Lazarus miracle will be a severe blow. Amongst many proofs brought forward in this cause, it has for obvious reasons played a role second only to the resurrection of Jesus himself. But an apologetic more sensitive to broadly accepted New Testament scholarship of recent times will look elsewhere than the miracles to set christological dogma upon a firm scriptural base.[14] In particular, it will attend to the faith of the early post-Easter community and note with what remarkable speed the members came to hold that the crucified Jesus of Nazareth was indeed uniquely Son of God - a process maturing in the gospel of John, but completed only some centuries later following the great christological controversies of the early church.[15]

In strictly Johannine terms we could perhaps fault the older apologetic for seeking to construct out of the miracle something of which the evangelist does not entirely approve. We have noted all along the ambivalent status accorded to "sign-faith" in the gospel. The miracles of Jesus do produce faith but not faith at a level required to really to "see the signs." In the Lazarus miracle it is "the Jews" who enact the apologetic approach, since they or at least some of them believe on the basis of the sign. But the full revelation comes to those who *bring* faith to the miracle, like Martha and, earlier, the mother of Jesus and the royal steward. They grasp the full revelation, of which the miracle itself is but symbol and sign. Such revelation concerns not just who Jesus was in himself (which is what the older apologetic principally sought to establish) but who he was and is *for* believers and the world.

Conclusion

The essential mission of Jesus in the Fourth Gospel is to be the agent of the Father in communicating life to the world. He communicates life by his teaching, but above all by revealing the glory of the Father. In the old dispensation no one could see God and live; the Israelites were warned not to approach the mountain (Sinai) lest they see the glory of God and perish. But to see the glory of God revealed in Jesus is precisely to find life.

Jesus reveals God's glory throughout his public life - in word and sign. But the culminating revelation comes on the cross: "When you have lifted up the Son of man, then you will know that I am He" (8:28a). Jesus is most "transparent" to the Godhead at this point in that his death upon the cross in self-sacrificing love reveals supremely that God "is love" (1 Jn 4:8). Paradoxically, then, it is above all in his own death that Jesus imparts life-giving revelation.

The Lazarus story, immediately preceding the Passion, powerfully enacts the truth that Jesus gives life at the cost of his own life. Our analysis of John 11 has shown how again and again the evangelist reminds us that Jesus puts his own life at mortal risk when he goes to Judea at the sisters' request. All comes to a climax in the scene before the tomb where we find Jesus torn between two powerful emotions: the love which impels him to work the sign and the shrinking from the prospect of his own death, an outcome which he knows the raising of Lazarus will bring on. Nothing could underline so clearly the cost to Jesus that communicating life incurs. Nothing could bring out so forcefully the love that impels the gift.

In this sense the narrative leading up to the raising of Lazarus can stand as a "parable" for the entire action of the Gospel. In chap. 11 we read that Jesus left his "safe country"—beyond the Jordan—to enter a territory of mortal danger—

Judea—in order to give life to a friend at the point of death. In the whole sweep of the Fourth Gospel the Word, who is "with God" (1:1, 2), "(ever) in the bosom of the Father" (1:18), leaves that "safe country" to come to a world which "God so loves" (3:16), but which is at the point of death because it has turned away from life. Though he comes to "his own," he enters a sphere of mortal danger because his own will know him not (1:10-11).

Within this wider view of John 11:1-46 Lazarus can stand as a typical or representative figure—a character with whom anyone who reads the Gospel can identify. "I" am Lazarus—in the sense that Jesus left his "safe country" (with the Father) to enter this world where he was at mortal danger in order to save me from death, to communicate—at the cost of his own life—eternal life to me. "I" am the "friend" of Jesus. "I" am "he (she) whom he loved". For "me" Jesus has wept. Before my tomb, so to speak, he has wrestled with the cost of life-giving love. It is to call me forth into life, to strip from me the bands of death that Jesus has come into the world and given his life.

So, with Lazarus, I am to contemplate the anointing of Jesus for burial (John 12:1-8). So, as one whom Jesus has brought back to life, I may experience, like Lazarus, the threat of persecution and death (12:10-11). But, above all, I am to read the account of the passion and death of Jesus (chaps. 12, 13-19) with intimate personal involvement, knowing that all this is being accepted by Jesus for love of me and to give life to me. I contemplate the supreme freedom and decisiveness of Jesus in the passion, knowing that behind it all stands a costly decision to give me life.

But Lazarus is not the only figure for personal identification in this episode. In the contrasting figures of Martha and Mary the evangelist addresses the human situation of all who are dismayed at the prospect or actuality of death. We have noted how strongly the evangelist underlines the motif of delay in setting out for Bethany. On hearing the sisters' appeal Jesus remains two days longer where he is and, in fact, lets Lazarus die (v. 6). Both sisters underline their sense of dismay by the remonstrance which each utters: "Lord, if you had been here, my brother would not have died" (v. 21, v. 32). Jesus loves and yet Jesus lets die. The Lord of life is not there when he is desperately needed. How can this absence be reconciled with love?

By so highlighting this apparent conflict between love and letting die, the Fourth Gospel accepts and legitimates the keen sense of God's absence felt by all believers who in grief confront the fact of death. The stark reality is not masked—we recall Jesus' bald assertion: "Lazarus is dead" (v. 14). No attempt here to smother the brutal fact with pious considerations of a conventional kind. On the contrary, the reality is accepted, the sense of God's absence acknowledged and an invitation given to set out with Martha on a journey of faith, a journey which proceeds from and accompanies as long as is necessary the full process of grief.

Normally present in human grieving and not unconnected with the sense of God's absence is an element of anger. As we have seen, anger features amongst the complex of Jesus' feelings as he goes to Lazarus' tomb. Jesus is angry before the fact of death—angry at Lazarus' death and the general grief it has caused, but angry too because giving life to his friend means confronting the prospect of death for himself. Has this depiction of Jesus as angry before death some bearing upon how grief should be handled within the context of faith? My sense is that it has. The Lazarus story in its own way gives permission for anger to be recognized, owned and expressed as an inescapable part of grief. Anger, conflict, struggle before the face of death is not inconsistent with faith. On the contrary, working through anger—as Jesus appears to work through his anger in this episode—is part of the journey in faith, the deepening of faith that confrontation with death requires.

Finally, Jesus weeps (v. 35). Jesus does not wail and mourn as do Mary and the Jews in their slender faith. The evangelist is careful to choose a different word. But Jesus weeps with and for the grieving family. In his weeping the divine weeps with and alongside the human, showing again the full compatibility between faith and genuine human sorrow.

Jesus, it is true, does in the end give back Lazarus to his grieving sisters. Christians reading the story in the context of recent bereavement will perhaps sense keenly that what Jesus did for Martha and Mary he has not done for them. But the miracle restores Lazarus simply to mortal human existence; he will die again. The lasting remedy to death occurs only within a context of a faith which has been led to see, beyond ordinary life and death, a life proceeding from Jesus which transcends these boundaries. Such a faith comes to see the raising of Lazarus not as a temporary remedy to the grieving of this particular family, but as a symbol of the eternal life communicated by Jesus to all believers.

The self-revelation of Jesus in John 11 meets a diverse response in terms of faith. Besides those who believe at various levels, there are also those—one group among "the Jews"—who do not come to faith at all. Unimpressed by the miracle, they go off to report the matter to the authorities and so set in train the process leading to Jesus' own death (v. 46). This negative response also enters into the total meaning of the narrative and requires consideration.

At first we are not told why "the Jews" take this action. But before long the real motivation emerges. The plot to do away with Jesus stems ultimately from fear of loss of power. The authorities correctly divine that because of this life-giving miracle "the whole world" is deserting them and going after Jesus (12:10-11, 19). The drama culminates in the trial before Pilate where Jesus is condemned plainly and openly because he is made out to pose a threat to Caesar (19:12). A helpless middle-man between the two forces, Caesar and "the Jews," Pilate hands over Jesus against his conscience because he sees what little power he has fast slipping from his grasp.

Jesus, the life-giver, is condemned to die because the giving of life threatens, challenges and dethrones the power structures of this world. "The Jews" who see the miracle but nonetheless go off to report the matter sense this all too well. Better simply to grieve and wail at death, to leave it untouched, unchallenged. For death can be an ally of power. Its overthrow, its defiance is always disturbing. Better to live in a gloomy world where at least one can wield a little influence for a time, rather than surrender to unpredictable, disturbing offers of life from God.

Seen in its full context, then, the raising of Lazarus illustrates the conflictual and costly aspect to the giving of life. God sent the Son to give life to the world, to break the grip of death. But that breaking involved "an aggressive conflict with the powers hostile to life."[1] Only at the cost of his own life could

Jesus give life. The cost stemmed not from some divine necessity or decree, but from the condition of a world that preferred the darkness. It is a cost that continues in those who, like Lazarus, are brought to life by Jesus. As they seek to follow him in discipleship and faith, they too come under threat (12:10-11). The forces of death cannot tolerate the living witnesses of life. Thomas, in this sense at least, accurately discerned the outcome (11:16).

The Lazarus narrative was undoubtedly framed for the Johannine community as it faced the increasing phenomenon of death in its own ranks. How could death have a place in what was supposed to be "the community of eternal life"?[2] How could Jesus somehow be "present", be "remaining" with the community, if members continued to die. It was presumably such painful questionings as these that led the community, or its leading theologian, to the distinction between "natural" and "eternal" life which runs through the entire narrative, becoming explicit in vv. 25-26. The Gospel does not hold both apart like two unconnected threads. Rather, it summons the believer to a faith which sees God's gift of "natural" life, even his miraculous restoration of it in the case of Lazarus, as a symbol of the "eternal life" which truly carries human destiny. Thus the story of Lazarus simply forms the culmination of what all the Johannine "signs" are attempting to do: lead believers to see the miraculous provision of "normal" human needs—wine, health, bread, sight, "natural" life itself—as symbols of the deeper life God is constantly holding out to human beings in Christ.

What the story of Lazarus provided for the first readers of the Fourth Gospel it continues to do for succeeding generations. Medical science and technology may prolong life. It may help people elude the grasp of death in many situations hitherto seen as fatal. But against all death lodges its undeniable claim. The same progress of science has helped us to see death as a natural process. But the primitive emotions aroused by death—the prospect of our own mortality, grief and dismay at the demise of others—remain just as strong. God lets us die and lets our loved ones die. Death, especially death that comes suddenly, prematurely, wantonly, remains the aspect of human existence that most challenges belief in the existence, sovereignty and goodness of God.

The story of Lazarus, with its full acceptance of human death and grieving, with its realism about the cost of giving life, with its invitation to enter upon a deeper journey of faith, speaks as powerfully to the present as it did to the past. God is neither indifferent to the distress death brings nor unsympathetic to our struggles of faith. More than anything else in the Gospel, Jesus' demeanor in John 11 expresses divine involvement in human grief and suffering. In the person of the Son God becomes vulnerable, physically and psychologically, to death. At its deepest level the story of Lazarus invites us to believe in God as the One who gives life in death and out of death. To every believer, confronted like Martha with mortality, Jesus addresses his words: "Did I not tell you that if you would believe you would see the glory of God?" (11:40).

I began this study contemplating Epstein's "Lazarus" in the antechapel of New College, Oxford. That sculpture is but one modern illustration of the powerful effect the story in John 11 has had in art and literature, as well as theology and religious belief, down the ages. To be released from the toils and bonds of death is a constant human aspiration. Deep within us all is the longing to hear an effective cry of liberation and summons to new life. Lazarus remains, then, a symbol of our hope for ourselves and our world. Our study may, I trust, have shown that we have a perfect right, indeed an invitation, to write ourselves, our world into the script—to be, each one of us, Lazarus, whom Jesus loved and for whom he gave his life.

Suggested Reading

Culpepper, R.A. *Anatomy of the Fourth Gospel: A Study in Literary Design* (Philadelphia: Fortress, 1983) 140-42, 149-202.

Dodd, C.H. *The Interpretation of the Fourth Gospel* (Cambridge: University Press, 1953) 363-68.

Fortna, R.T. *The Fourth Gospel and Its Predecessor. From Narrative Source to Present Gospel* (Philadelphia: Fortress, 1988) 94-109.

Henneberry, B.H. *The Raising of Lazarus (John 11:1-44): An Evaluation of the Hypothesis that a Written Tradition Lies Behind the Narrative.* Ann Arbor: University Microfilms, 1984.

Kremer, J. *Lazarus: Die Geschichte einer Auferstehung: Text, Wirkungsgeschichte und Botschaft.* Stuttgart: Kath. Bibelwerk, 1985.

Kysar, R. *John: The Maverick Gospel* (Atlanta: John Knox, 1976) 67-73, 84-93.

Martin, J.P. "History and Eschatology in the Lazarus Narrative, John 11, 1-44," *SJT* 17 (1964) 332-43.

Moule, C.F.D. "The Meaning of 'Life' in the Gospels and Epistles of John: A Study in the Story of Lazarus. John 11:1-44," *Theology* 78 (1975) 114-25.

Rochais, G. *Les récits de résurrection des morts dans le Nouveau Testament.* SNTSMS 40 (Cambridge: University Press, 1981) 113-46.

Schnackenburg, R. "The Lazarus story: the formation of the tradition and the historical problems" in *The Gospel according to St. John.* Vol 2 (London: Burns & Oates, 1980) 340-46.

Schneiders, S.M. "Death in the Community of Eternal Life: History, Theology and Spirituality in John 11," *Interpretation* 41 (1987) 44-56.

Endnotes

Notes, Introduction

[1]See E. Becker, *The Denial of Death* (New York: The Free Press, 1973), 11-24 (Chap 2: "The Terror of Death").

[2]Ibid. p. 12.

[3]See, e. g., Descamps, A. -L. (et alii), *Genèse et Structure d'un Texte du Nouveau Testament: étude interdisciplinaire du chapître 11 de l'Evangile de Jean.* Lectio Divina 104. Paris/Louvain: Cerf/Cabay, 1981 (all the contributions, save those of A.-L. Descamps and J. Ponthot, adopt a structuralist approach); Jones, J. R., *Narrative Structures and Meaning in John 11:1-54.* Ann Arbor: University Microfilms, 1982.

Notes, Chapter 1

[1]The committal of the Fourth Gospel to writing may in fact have occurred at the time of the death of the Beloved Disciple.

[2]For a comprehensive critical survey of the "Signs Source" hypothesis see R. Kysar, *The Fourth Evangelist and His Gospel: An Examination of Contemporary Scholarship* (Minneapolis: Augsburg, 1975) 13-37.

[3]It may well be that we hear the original ending of such a document at the close of chap. 20: "Now Jesus did many other signs in the presence of the disciples, which are not written in this book; but these are written that you may believe that Jesus is the Christ, the Son of God, and that believing you may have life in his name" (vv. 30-31).

[4]Scholars, however, have looked about for a further, seventh sign to complete the sacred number. Jesus' walking on the water (6:19-21) has been regarded as a sign. Its inclusion in the list would, appropriately, make the raising of Lazarus the seventh and final sign. But the walking on the water is more a private act of Jesus, conferring no notable benefit upon others as do the remaining signs. In chap. 3 of this present work, in connection with the appearance of Lazarus as he emerges from the tomb, I shall discuss the possibility that the arrangement of the grave clothes in Jesus' empty tomb constitutes a sign for the Beloved Disciple, leading him to faith in the resurrection.

[5]For a most lucid outline of Johannine eschatology see R. Kysar, *John: the Maverick Gospel* (Atlanta: John Knox, 1976) 84-92.

[6]On the Johannine misunderstandings see esp. R.A. Culpepper, *Anatomy of the Fourth Gospel* (Philadelphia: Fortress, 1983) 152-65.

[7]On Irony cf. ibid. 165-80.

[8]Cf. C.H. Dodd, *The Interpretation of the Fourth Gospel* (Cambridge: Cambridge University Press, 1953) 289-91. Some scholars, e.g. R.E. Brown, (*The Gospel according to John I-XII* [AB 29; New York: Doubleday, 1966] cxxxviii-cxliv) see the "Book of Signs" as beginning already with the testimony of the Baptist (1:19). There is much to be said for this but personally I feel it is best to see the "Book of Signs" as beginning with the first sign, the first Cana miracle (2:1-11).

Notes, Chapter 2

[1]Cf. J. Kremer, *Lazarus: Die Geschichte einer Auferstehung: Text, Wirkungsgeschichte und Botschaft* (Stuttgart: Kath. Bibelwerk, 1985) 29, 31.

[2]The Nain miracle also has affinities with miracles "upon the road" told of miracle-working figures in the Greco-Roman world; see G. Rochais, *Les récits de resurrection des morts dans la Nouveau Testament* (Cambridge: University Press, 1981) 19-21.

Notes, Chapter 3

[1]The form of their plea recalls the first Cana sign, where the mother of Jesus similarly invokes his help by simply pointing to the fact: "They have no wine" (2:3).

[2]This is sharply to take issue with Brown, *John I-XII* 423, who regards v. 5 as merely an unnecessary gloss.

[3]In somewhat similar fashion Jesus in chap. 9 accounts for the condition of the man born blind as due neither to his own sin or that of his parents but "that the works of God might be made manifest in him" (v. 3).

[4]"Thomas is the model of the disciple who understands Jesus' flesh but not his glory" (Culpepper, *Anatomy of the Fourth Gospel* 123).

[5]Cf. R. Bultmann, *The Gospel of John: A Commentary* (Oxford: Blackwell, 1971) 401, n. 8; Brown, *John I-XII* 424.

[6]For the posture see Job 2:8, 13; Ezek 8:14.

[7]Cf. Bultmann, *John* 401.

[8]With the phrase, " . . . even if he dies," the evangelist may be confronting in first instance the dismay caused by the increasing phenomenon of death within the Johannine community; cf. J. P. Martin, "History and Eschatology in the Lazarus Narrative, John 11, 1-44," *Scottish Journal of Theology* 17 (1964) 332-43.

[9]Cf. esp. R. Schnackenburg, *The Gospel according to St. John* (3 vols.; New York: Crossroad, 1968, 1979, 1982) 2.330. Jesus' response here forms a close parallel to a similar move made in the dialogue with the Samaritan woman at the well (4:1-42). Preoccupied with her need to draw ordinary water from the well, she looks to Jesus as one who may be able to solve that problem on a permanent basis miraculously (4:15). But Jesus moves her away from fixation on the need for ordinary water. He leads her to see it as merely a symbol of a vastly more significant need for "living water" (the life-giving revelation) which he has to offer (vv. 13-15). The water she wants will only solve her thirst for a time; she will thirst again. He can offer her "living water," to slake an eternal thirst. Similarly, in the discourse in John 6 the Jewish crowd want Jesus to provide them with ordinary food on a regular basis by repeating, as a new Moses, the miracle of the manna (6:30, 31, 34). Jesus warns them not to "labor" for (ordinary) food, which perishes—as even the miraculously given manna perished, but to labor for the truly life-giving "Bread from heaven" which he himself is (vv. 27, 32-33). Again he moves from the situation of human need—and the immediate miraculous remedy it seems to call for—to an ultimate lasting remedy which he, uniquely, can provide.

[10]That is, understanding the "lives" here to refer to ordinary human life (as Bultmann, *John* 403; C. K. Barrett, *The Gospel According to St. John* [2d ed.; London: SPCK, 1978] 396; Schnackenburg, *John* 2.331, 515), rather than to eternal life or the life of faith, in strict agreement with the "will live" of the preceding sentence (as Dodd, *Interpretation* 365; Brown, *John I-XII* 434). The latter interpretation has problems with "believes" since logically it should precede "lives" taken in this sense. The double sense of "lives" corresponds to the double sense of "dies."

[11]So most modern scholars: see, e.g., Bultmann, *John* 404, n.5; Schnackenburg, *John* 2.332; Barrett, *John* 396-97; B. Lindars, *The Gospel of John* (New Century; Grand Rapids: Eerdmans, 1981) 396; B. H. Henneberry, *The Raising of Lazarus (John 11:1-44): An Evaluation of the Hypothesis that a Written Tradition Lies Behind the Narrative* (Ann Arbor: University Microfilms, 1984)144; Rochais, *Les récits* 143; Kremer, *Lazarus* 70-71.

[12]For this view, see amongst recent commentators, Brown, *John I-XII* 434; F. J. Moloney, *The Word Became Flesh* (Cork: Mercier, 1977) 64-65, who, in addition to other considerations we have noted, points out how Martha when she summons her sister shortly after (v. 28) refers to Jesus as "the Teacher."

[13]Cf. especially the lucid discussion by Barrett, *John* 399-400.

[14]In the synoptic account of the raising of Jairus' daughter, Jesus rebukes and expels from the scene the professional mourners and wailers (Matt 13:23-25); Mark 5:38-40; Luke 8:52-53).

[15]Nor is the anger sufficiently explained, as has been also suggested, by confrontation with the power of death personified. Such a view of death, familiar from Paul, is not found in the Fourth Gospel.

[16]For a similar interpretation see Barrett, *John* 399; Brown, *John I-XII* 425-26, 435.

[17]"The spices with which the Jewish people normally prepared a body for burial were sufficient only to allay the odor of decomposition until burial and did not constitute a real embalmment as that practiced by the Egyptians. By the fourth day these spices would have had no effect on a decomposing body" (Henneberry, *The Raising of Lazarus* 181).

[18]Cf. Schnackenburg (*John* 2.339), citing W. Lütgert: "It is because he is one with God that he prays and because he prays he is one with God."

[19]I have developed this more fully in an earlier study, "The Faith of the Beloved Disciple and the Community in John 20," *Journal for the Study of the New Testament* 23 (1985) 83-97.

[20]The suggestion has been made that Lazarus continues in the gospel in the person of the "Beloved Disciple" who plays such a prominent role in the events of the passion and risen life of Jesus (13:23-25; cf. 18:16; 19:26-27; 19:35-37; 20:2-10; 21:7, 20-23, 24). Certainly, we are again and again reminded in John 11 that Jesus loves Lazarus and the episode at the empty tomb (20:2-10), in which the Beloved Disciple plays a leading role has, as argued above, clear links with the raising of Lazarus. But I would in the end agree with the judgment of R. H. Culpepper on this matter: "Although one can readily understand why Lazarus might have the place of honor at the last supper and why the brethren might think he would not die, it is not sufficiently clear that the gospel intends this identification" (*Anatomy of the Fourth Gospel* 141, n. 84.).

Notes Chapter 4

[1]Cf. Rochais, *Les récits* 115-21.

[2]This basically corresponds to the "consensus" reconstruction set out by B.H. Henneberry as a result of his exhaustive survey of scholarly attempts to separate tradition and redaction in the Lazarus narrative (*The Raising of Lazarus* 63-64). I have, however, included more of v. 33 (the reference to Jesus' emotional reaction) than Henneberry. Some scholars distinguish between this basic text and the final form of John 11:1-44 an intermediate stage which contained further elements now appearing in v. 7, v. 11, v. 12, v. 14 and v. 33: see, e.g., Kremer, *Lazarus* 86-89; Rochais, *Les*

récits 123, 129; this intermediate text they would assign to the "Book of Signs"; earlier, Bultmann, *John* 395-96, n. 4.

[3]For a comprehensive critical survey of the "Signs Source" hypothesis see R. Kysar, *The Fourth Evangelist and His Gospel: An Examination of Contemporary Scholarship* (Minneapolis: Augsburg, 1975) 13-37.

[4]Henneberry is skeptical even about the existence of a written source: "At most, if there was a written tradition behind the story, it would have to have been one which was read earlier by the evangelist and was used so completely in his composition of the story that it is now impossible to identify it or even to be certain of its existence" (*The Raising of Lazarus* 203).

[5]The evidence of this is set out in J. M. Creed, *The Gospel according to St. Luke* (London: Macmillan, 1930) 318-21.

[6]Cf. Kremer, *Lazarus* 95-109.

[7]For a brief summary of this see N. Perrin and D. Duling, *The New Testament: An Introduction* (2d ed.; New York, etc.: Harcourt, Brace, Jovanovich, 1982) 407-08. G. Vermes, *Jesus the Jew* (London: Collins, 1973) 69-82, sets the miracle-working of Jesus within the context of similar claims made for other Galilean charismatic figures, roughly contemporary with Jesus (notably Honi ["The Circle Drawer"] and Hanina ben Dosa) in Jewish literature.

[8]See especially Rochais, *Les récits* 39-32.

[9]It is impossible for us to verify historically that the child really was dead and not simply in some sort of coma mistaken for death; in the account, Jesus himself seems to play down the miracle by asserting that the child is merely sleeping (v. 39). On this see again Rochais, *Les récits* 110.

[10]In the gospel tradition we would seem to have illustrations of this when we compare John's presentation of the episode with the royal steward in 4:46-54 and the synoptic tradition of the cure of the centurion's servant (Matt 8:5-13 parallel Luke 7:1-10), with which it is evidently related; cf. also the Johannine and the synoptic accounts of the feeding of the multitude (John 6:1-15; Mark 6:35-44 and parallels); on this tendency cf. Kremer, *Lazarus* 106.

[11]For a survey of this view see Henneberry, *The Raising of Lazarus* pp. xv-xix.

[12]See B. Byrne, "Forceful Stewardship and Neglectful Wealth: A Contemporary Reading of Luke 16," *Pacifica* 1 (1988) 1-14, esp. pp. 5-9.

[13]Cf. Kremer, *Lazarus 107.*

[14]See A. Dulles, *Apologetics and the Biblical Christ* (London: Burns & Oates, 1964), esp. 80-95; R.E. Brown, *Jesus God and Man* (London: Chapman, 1968).

[15]Cf. C.F.D. Moule, *The Origin of Christology* (Cambridge: Cambridge University, 1977); J.D.G. Dunn, *Christology in the Making* (London: SCM, 1980).

Notes, Conclusion

[1]C.H. Dodd, *The Interpretation of the Fourth Gospel* (Cambridge: Cambridge University, 1953) 262.

[2]The phrase is taken from the title of S.M. Schneiders' perceptive study of John 11 from the point of view of history, theology and spirituality: "Death in the Community of Eternal Life: History, Theology and Spirituality in John 11," *Interpretation* 41 (1987) 44-56.